12-Step Programs

Stanice Anderson

12-Step Programs

A Resource Guide for Helping Professionals

Stanice Anderson

ISBN 1-55691-163-7

Learning Publications, Inc.
5351 Gulf Drive
P.O. Box 1338
Holmes Beach, FL 34218-1338

Printing: 5 4 3 2 1   Year: 3 2 1 0 9

Printed in the United States of America.

Dedication

In loving memory of my father, Stanley James Anderson, Sr.

Contents

Other Types of Step-Fellowship Programs

Acknowledgments

A special offering of thanksgiving to God who provided everything I needed, including my dad's "people gene," to complete this book and send it out into the world.

I thank my son, best friend, and inspiration, Michael Tucker, Jr., who loved me right on up to the finish line. I thank my mother, Virginia Anderson, who dealt with mountains of mail and a perpetual stream of telephone calls. I thank the rest of my family, each with their own flavor of encouragement and love.

I thank my friends that love, encourage, and believe in me: Dorine Phelps, Delphine Glaze, Carol Powers, Claudia Holloway, Helen Smith, BJ Connor, Vaughn DeCarlos, Joyce Williams, Albert McNeil, Michael Sr., Katherine, and Mary Ann Tucker; Bishop Meyers, Herbert and Thelma Smith, Pastor Finny, Charles Walker, LeBarry Williams, Tressa Jackson and Michele Jones. I thank my friends since childhood Omie Brown, Cynthia Dawkins, Peggy, and Pat Stroman for their acceptance and unconditional love.

I thank my editor and friend Tamara Holmes, assistant editor, USATODAY.com who in her not-so-spare time edited my manuscript before I submited it; thereby, giving me an edge. Thanks for the edge, Tamara.

I thank Tom Fuller, a dear friend, and my writing teacher, who shared with me his love for the art of the written word.

I thank my cheerleaders at USATODAY and USATODAY.com: Lois McFarland, Lee Ivory, Carol Colclaser, Gloria Ryan, Tracy Moran, Katie O'Brien, Andrea Smith, Lawan McFerren, Tim Bendel, and Boots Rykiel.

I thank The 700 Club, Steve Wright, Drs. Mitch Huggonet and G. Ray Coleman, and Marie Logan. I'll never forget how much you've helped me. My spirit reaches out to touch and thank the spirits of those that started this journey with me but who didn't get to see the completed book: My dad, Stanley Anderson; Rev. John Kinard, Gloria Hardy, Tina Teasley, and Jazz. I miss you now but I'll love you forever!

A special thanks to all of the 12-step programs that gave me permission to reprint material in the directory portion of this book.

I thank Ruth and Edsel Erickson, my publishers at Learning Publications, Inc. who believed in my work enough to take a risk to publish. I also thank Vicki DiOrazio, Production Manager, for her professionalism and assuring manner.

TOGETHER, we have accomplished what I could not have accomplished alone!

Preface

Twelve-Step Programs: A Resource Guide for Helping Professionals is the result of personal participation in 12-step programs. I have witnessed, firsthand, the tremendous life-changing power of 12-step programs in my own life and thousands of other lives. Through embracing two of these programs, in particular I have been able to break free of the grip and vicious cycle of active drug and alcohol addiction and have remained clean and sober for over 14 years. Support is available. The programs work.

Another vital source of help for me came from caring professionals who treated me like a person and not just another number or unwanted client on their caseload. They helped me face the fact that I did have a serious problem that I could not beat alone. The river of denial runs deep.

I knew this book had to be written after I received a telephone call late one night from a man who was given my business card by a friend. Although he wished to remain anonymous, he did reveal to me that he was in an unhealthy relationship with a woman who emotionally and verbally abused him. He had been trying to break free from this relationship for over two years — but to no avail. He had even sought and received professional help; however, he still found it impossible to sever the relationship.

This man told me that he felt so powerless in his situation. He had heard of the 12-step programs, Alcoholics Anonymous, and Narcotics Anonymous. He told me that he was not addicted to drugs or alcohol.

However, he painfully admitted to me that he felt hopelessly addicted to a woman and the abuse that she heaped upon him. He was sick and tired of living his life in quiet desperation, feeling he was alone in this type of situation. He wanted to know if there was a 12-step program that existed that could provide additional support.

At the time, I knew of one particular program that might fit his needs: I suggested he attend a meeting of Sex and Love Addicts Anonymous. He was relieved to find out that he was not the only person in the world struggling with such feelings. It was that night that the idea for the *12-Step Programs: A Resource Guide for Helping Professionals* was born.

Through speaking engagements and conducting workshops, I have had the opportunity to meet and talk with many people across the United States — helping professionals, family members, people who are suffering, as well as thousands of people who have found recovery through 12-step programs. Over the years, I have received many telephone calls with questions about 12-step programs. Whether it is to appropriately refer patients, clients, loved ones, or in most cases, for themselves, people want and need to know what 12-step programs exist, which ones would benefit them, and how to contact these programs.

Many helping professionals have heard of Alcoholics Anonymous, Narcotics Anonymous, and even Gamblers Anonymous. But what about Sex and Love Addicts Anonymous, Helping CrossDressers Anonymous, Fear of Success Anonymous, or Self-Mutilators Anonymous? Even if you have heard of such organizations, how many know which program is appropriate?

How and why should helping professionals refer someone to a program that they know little or nothing about? The answers to these questions and more are found in this guide.

Many resources are available that explore different aspects of the recovery process; however, the recovery community lacks a resource guide with specific insider's details about 12-step meetings, starting 12-step groups, and a list of 60 plus 12-step programs complete with headquarters' locations, telephone numbers, email and website addresses. This information makes this book unique. The text also includes self-assessment questions — with written permission granted — formulated by the 12-step programs.

Some programs were omitted because they have not survived or were about to go out of existence due to lack of participation. Maybe, if more people know that these programs exist and how to contact them, more can survive. If you know of a 12-step program that you do not see listed and would like to see listed in the next edition, please write me in care of the publisher.

Two words sum up why this book is timely and necessary — managed care. Managed care limits office visits to such a degree that an additional mechanism must be in place to assure the sustained support that people need to recover.

1
Introduction

There are countless people suffering emotional, mental, and spiritual anguish because of addictions that they feel cannot be overcome or other problems that just seem insurmountable. They feel hopelessness and despair, and perhaps worst of all, they feel alone in their trouble. No one knows this more than helping professionals. These people come into your office seeking help and get it; but some do not have the support, empathy, or the hope they can get from other people who suffer from the same malady. After the therapy or counseling session is over, many can walk out of your office and still feel alone in their struggle.

There are tens of thousands of men, women, and children living their lives in quiet desperation. People are suffering as a direct result of addiction, compulsive behaviors, and lifestyle problems. Many of these people and the people who love them do not even realize that there is additional help available through 12-step programs. If you are a helping professional who would like to know exactly what 12-step groups are available and the inner workings of these programs, so that you may feel confident about referring people to the additional support that is available, this book is for you.

On these pages, you will find the most comprehensive information available about 12-step programs. My hope is that this resource guide will prove invaluable to helping professionals. Not only does it list over 60 12-step programs, it also offers an insiders' look at how the programs are able to help millions of people. This guide provides a comprehensive directory of support programs, complete with addresses, telephone numbers, email addresses (where available), Internet website addresses (where available), summaries of each program, and a list of self-assessment questions to help the caregiver identify whether or not a particular program is applicable. There also are chapters on meetings and start-up procedures. The more information you are armed with, the better prepared you are to help people find a new way of life.

Helping professionals routinely refer people to the more widely known 12-step programs, such as Alcoholics Anonymous and Narcotics Anonymous. There is a great deal lot of information readily available within the helping professional community about these two programs. Sometimes people referred to these programs go to the meetings and decide that the program is not for them. Most often it is simply a matter of denial; however, there are instances where the program that they are referred to really does not address a particular need. Identification is the key. Can the client identify with the program's purpose and goal? A lack of information is one reason that these referrals are not more tailored to the person's actual needs. Many of the 12-step programs are not common knowledge.

I have over 14 years of personal and professional experience with 12-step programs. Professionally, I have worked as a counselor and a representative for treatment centers and transitional-care programs. I have also written articles and designed and conducted workshops on 12-step programs and the addiction-recovery process.

One thing I have learned during these years in active participation in the recovery process, both as a helping professional and a person in recovery, is that there's always hope. No person, no situation, no circumstance is hopeless. I pray this resource guide will renew your hope for the people you seek to help. Hope is contagious. You get it and you cannot help but pass it on. That's just the way it is.

2
How to Get the Most Out of this Resource Guide

The following suggestions should help you get the most out of this resource guide:

- Determine the 12-step program(s) you would like to know more about. Call or write for more information, including meeting availability and locations in your area. Where available, email and Internet addresses are provided. Some of the programs contacted were willing to provide a first name and telephone number of a contact person in the given geographic area.

- When requesting information by mail, send a self-addressed, stamped envelope, as most of these programs are non-profit organizations.

- If there are no meetings in your immediate area, request a "group-starter kit." The kit contains all the information necessary to start a group. For instance, finding a location, getting the word out to the public, what literature is needed, choosing a format, as well as step-by-step directions on how to conduct a meeting. However, it is suggested that before starting a new group, you go to a few of the meetings of any 12-step program that is available in your area. Although each program has a different focus, the meetings are conducted using a similar format and structure.

- If starting a new meeting where the 12-step program already exists, you may want to enlist the help of at least one "old timer." An "old timer" is a person with multiple years of experience as an active member in a 12-step program; this experience will prove to be an invaluable asset in getting the new meeting started, focused, and on track.

- When making a referral to a 12-step program, suggest that a client attend a minimum of six meetings before making a decision on whether to continue participation.

- Self-assessment questions for some of the 12-step programs are included in this book. These 12-step programs' formulated self-assessment questions are based on their common and combined experiences. Before you make a referral, go over these questions with the client to make sure that the program under consideration is appropriate. Most of the program self-assessment questions and other literature are copyrighted, therefore, pamphlets containing the questions should be ordered directly from the 12-step programs.

- Order a supply of pamphlets, program texts (audio books also available), and speakers tapes. These can be used during a session, given or loaned to clients.

- Provide your clients with information and encourage them to attend 12-step program meetings.

- Plant as many seeds of recovery as possible. It is not your business if and when these seeds grow — your task is to simply plant the seeds.

What Are 12-Step Programs?

Twelve-step programs are nonprofit organizations that are made up of peer groups of people who provide emotional and spiritual support for one another. These programs are for people who are living unhealthy lifestyles and want to make a change for the better. Whether the unhealthy lifestyle is a result of addictions, past traumas, divorce, physical or mental problems, 12-step programs have helped millions of people turn their lives around.

Alcoholics Anonymous was the first 12-step program. The 12-step programs that have since emerged, must secure permission from Alcoholics Anonymous to reprint and adapt the "12 steps" and the "12 traditions" to their particular focus. The steps and traditions are listed on pages 6 and 7.

Twelve-step programs are referred to as "fellowships" because each program is comprised of a community of people with a common problem, as well as a shared interest in recovering from that problem. The primary goal of 12-step programs is to find solutions to common problems and help others find recovery.

This goal is accomplished through members sharing their stories, experiences, strengths, and hopes with one another. There is a therapeutic value in someone who has "been there" helping someone who is presently "there." Together, they seem to do what one individual cannot do alone — recover.

Twelve-step programs seek to provide an environment in which recovery is possible. This environment is created and safeguarded by the 12 traditions; especially the principle of "anonymity." Each of the program titles includes the word, *anonymous*, and members identify themselves by their first names only because: *Anonymity is the spiritual foundation of all our traditions ever reminding us to place principles before personalities* (12th Tradition).

The "tools of recovery," common to all of the 12-step programs, include:

- Meetings (usually 60 - 90 minutes)
- Sponsorship
- Twelve steps
- Twelve traditions
- Service work

These tools are believed to be necessary to affect the personality change needed to nurture and sustain the recovery process; they also help to enhance the quality of life of the recovering person, as well as the people whose lives they touch.

Twelve-step programs **are not** to be confused with therapeutic counseling groups; nor should they be utilized as a substitute for professional help. Twelve-step programs can, however, provide the long-range peer support necessary to sustain recovery. Given the necessary information, the helping professional is well-placed to recommend the appropriate program to meet the client's need.

The 12 Steps of Alcoholics Anonymous*

1. We admitted we were powerless over alcohol — that our lives had become unmanageable.

2. Came to believe that a Power greater than ourselves could restore us to sanity.

3. Made a decision to turn our will and our lives over to the care of God, as we understood Him.

4. Made a searching and fearless moral inventory of ourselves.

5. Admitted to God, to ourselves, and to another human being the exact nature of our wrongs.

6. Were entirely ready to have God remove all these defects of character.

7. Humbly asked Him to remove our shortcomings.

8. Made a list of all persons we had harmed, and became willing to make amends to them all.

9. Made direct amends to such people wherever possible, except when to do so would injure them or others.

10. Continued to take personal inventory and when we were wrong promptly admitted it.

11. Sought through prayer and meditation to improve our conscious contact with God, as we understood Him, praying only for knowledge of His will for us and the power to carry that out.

12. Having had a spiritual awakening as the result of these steps, we tried to carry this message to alcoholics, and to practice these principles in all our affairs.

*The 12 Steps, 12 Traditions, and brief excerpts are reprinted with permission of Alcoholics Anonymous World Services, Inc. Permission to reprint this material does not mean that A.A. has reviewed or approved the contents of this publication, nor that A.A. agrees with the views expressed herein. A.A. is a program of recovery from alcoholism only — use of these excerpts in connection with programs and activities which are patterned after A.A., but which address other problems, or in any other non-A.A. context, does not imply otherwise.

The 12 Traditions of Alcoholics Anonymous*

1. Our common welfare should come first; personal recovery depends upon A.A. unity.

2. For our group purpose there is but one ultimate authority — a loving God as He may express Himself in our group conscience. Our leaders are but trusted servants; they do not govern.

3. The only requirement for A.A. membership is a desire to stop drinking.

4. Each group should be autonomous except in matters affecting other groups or A.A. as a whole.

5. Each group has but one primary purpose — to carry its message to the alcoholic who still suffers.

6. An A.A. group ought never endorse, finance, or lend the A.A. name to any related facility or outside enterprise lest problems of money, property, and prestige divert us from our primary purpose.

7. Every A.A. group ought to be fully self-supporting declining outside contributions.

8. Alcoholics Anonymous should remain forever nonprofessional but our service centers may employ special workers.

9. A.A., as such, ought never be organized; but we may create service boards or committees directly responsible to those they serve.

10. Alcoholics Anonymous has no opinion on outside issues; hence the A.A. name ought never be drawn into public controversy.

11. Our public relations policy is based on attraction rather than promotion; we need always maintain personal anonymity at the level of press, radio, and films.

12. Anonymity is the spiritual foundation of all our Traditions, ever reminding us to place principles before personalities.

---

*The 12 Steps, 12 Traditions, and brief excerpts are reprinted with permission of Alcoholics Anonymous World Services, Inc. Permission to reprint this material does not mean that A.A. has reviewed or approved the contents of this publication, nor that A.A. agrees with the views expressed herein. A.A. is a program of recovery from alcoholism only — use of these excerpts in connection with programs and activities which are patterned after A.A., but which address other problems, or in any other non-A.A. context, does not imply otherwise.

For a better understanding of the benefits that can result from "living" the 12 Steps and 12 Traditions that are the foundation of the "program," we go to the source, the text of what is generally known in 12-step circles as *The Big Book* which is actually entitled: *Alcoholics Anonymous*. These are the promises from Chapter 6, Into Action.

"The spiritual life is not a theory. We have to live it. Unless one's family expresses a desire to live upon spiritual principles we think we ought not to urge them. We should not talk incessantly to them about spiritual matters. They will change in time. Our behavior will convince them more than our words. We must remember that 10 or 20 years of drunkenness would make a skeptic out of anyone.

"There may be some wrongs we can never fully right. We do not worry about them if we can honestly say to ourselves that we would right them if we could. Some people cannot be seen — we sent them an honest letter. And there may be a valid reason for postponement in some cases. But we do not delay if it can be avoided. We should be sensible, tactful, considerate, and humble without being servile or scraping. As God's people we stand on our feet; we do not crawl before anyone.

"If we are painstaking about this phase of our development, we will be amazed before we are half way through. We are going to know a new freedom and a new happiness. We will not regret the past nor wish to shut the door on it. We will comprehend the word serenity and we will know peace. No matter how far down the scale we have gone, we will see how our experience can benefit others. That feeling of uselessness and self-pity will disappear. We will lose interest in selfish things and gain interest in our fellows. Self-seeking will slip away. Our whole attitude and outlook upon life will change. Fear of people and of economic insecurity will leave us. We will intuitively know how to handle situations which used to baffle us. We will suddenly realize that God is doing for us what we could not do for ourselves.

"Are these extravagant promises? We think not. They are being fulfilled among us — sometimes quickly, sometimes slowly. They will always materialize if we work for them." (*Alcoholics Anonymous* 1976).

---

*Alcoholics Anonymous, 3rd ed., 1976, p. 83-4. The 12 Steps, 12 Traditions, and brief excerpts are reprinted with permission of Alcoholics Anonymous World Services, Inc. Permission to reprint this material does not mean that A.A. has reviewed or approved the contents of this publication, nor that A.A. agrees with the views expressed herein. A.A. is a program of recovery from alcoholism only — use of these excerpts in connection with programs and activities which are patterned after A.A., but which address other problems, or in any other non-A.A. context, does not imply otherwise.

3
12-Step Meetings

What Are 12-Step Meetings?

Twelve-step meetings are one of the primary "tools of recovery." Twelve-step programs are comprised of groups that meet at designated times and days of the week. Some groups meet more than once per week. The more widely known programs such as Alcoholics Anonymous (A.A.) and Narcotics Anonymous (NA) have hundreds of thousands of groups meeting nationally and internationally.

Meetings have various formats. Generally, meetings open with the reading of the program's preamble, a description of the common problem, as well as the proposed solution. To help you understand how the ideas of 12-step recovery programs are adapted from a common source, here is the preamble of Alcoholics Anonymous followed by the preamble for CoDependents Anonymous (CoDA):

Alcoholics Anonymous Preamble:* "Alcoholics Anonymous is a fellowship of women and men who share their experience, strength, and hope with each other that they may solve their common problem and help others to recover from alcoholism.

"The only requirement for membership is a desire to stop drinking. There are no dues or fees for A.A. membership; we are self-supporting through our own contributions.

"A.A. is not allied with any sect, denomination, politics, organization, or institution; does not wish to engage in any controversy, neither endorses nor opposes any causes. Our primary purpose is to stay sober and help other alcoholics to achieve sobriety." (*Alcoholics Anonymous,* 1976).

**Alcoholics Anonymous,* 3rd ed., 1976. The 12 Steps, 12 Traditions, and brief excerpts are reprinted with permission of Alcoholics Anonymous World Services, Inc. Permission to reprint this material does not mean that A.A. has reviewed or approved the contents of this publication, nor that A.A. agrees with the views expressed herein. A.A. is a program of recovery from alcoholism only — use of these excerpts in connection with programs and activities which are patterned after A.A., but which address other problems, or in any other non-A.A. context, does not imply otherwise.

*Co-Dependents Anonymous (CoDA) Preamble:** "CoDependents Anonymous is a fellowship of men and women whose common purpose is to develop healthy relationships. The only requirement for membership is a desire for healthy and fulfilling relationships. We gather together to support and share with each other in a journey of self-discovery — learning to love the self. Living the program allows each of us to become increasingly honest with ourselves about our personal histories and our own codependent behaviors.

"We rely upon the 12 Steps and 12 Traditions for knowledge and wisdom. These are the principles of our program and guides to developing honest and fulfilling relationships with ourselves and others. In CoDA, we each learn to build a bridge to a Higher Power of our own understanding, and we allow others the same privilege.

"This renewal process is a gift of healing for us. By actively working the program of CoDependents Anonymous, we can each realize a new joy, acceptance, and serenity in our lives."

The Opening Prayer of CoDependents Anonymous*

In the spirit of love and truth, we ask our Higher Power
To guide us as we share our experience, strength, and hope.

We open our hearts to the light of wisdom,
The warmth of love, and the joy of acceptance.

It is also common that the program's 12 steps and/or 12 traditions are read. Throughout the 12-step community, it is understood that all it takes is two or more people to have a meeting. The number of people in attendance is secondary. The primary purpose of any meeting is to give and receive a message of hope that recovery is possible. The message is carried when people who share a common problem come together in a meeting to share their experiences, strengths, and hopes with one another. Going to these meetings regularly starts the process of recovery.

After the opening readings, some groups have an experienced member share his or her "story." A member's story usually describes what life was like before coming to the program; what set of circumstances and feelings brought them to seek help from the program; and what he or she has experienced since coming into the program. Hopefully, the member's story helps newcomers identify with the feelings more so than the experiences and come to the realization that they, too, can recover. The proc-

---

*Reprinted by permission of CoDA Board of Trustees. From CoDependents Anonymous website. Conference approved 9/31/91.

ess also helps the storyteller remember where he or she has been and where he or she wants to go. Understanding one's own history is important so that people will not continue with behaviors that will only result in the repeating of that history. If nothing changes, nothing changes. Understanding is also the fertile ground where an attitude of gratitude can grow. Gratitude affects the recovery process in a positive way.

Next, the speaker or someone in attendance usually suggests a discussion topic. Examples of topics include:

- Gratitude
- Sponsorship
- Staying focused one day at a time
- Honesty and how it affects recovery
- Recovery and relapse
- Living life on life's terms
- What lengths are you willing to go to recover?

The meeting is then opened for sharing by anyone in attendance. Everyone in the meeting is free to talk about the topic, or about any urgent problems, and/or living situations they may be experiencing.

"Share" is the term 12-steppers use to describe the act of verbally communicating with another their feelings and experiences of the moment or the past, problems and solutions, fears or hopes, and defeats or victories. Cross talk is not allowed because 12-steppers are encouraged to "learn to listen and listen to learn." If someone at the meeting can relate to what is shared, they may, in turn, share similar experiences or feelings; this "sharing" process allows everyone to witness that they are not alone in what they feel or whatever situation they may find themselves. Together, solutions are found. Feelings of alienation and isolation begin to slip away. There is a real therapeutic value in people with a common problem sharing with one another; there is something special about hearing and interacting with other people, who have done that, been there, and gotten through it. Through this sharing process, people come to believe that they can get through anything, with the help of others, without going back to the destructive behavior that brought them to the point of desperation in the first place.

Meetings also provide a safe haven, for example, if a person is recovering from alcohol or drug addiction, there maybe times when he or she has an overwhelming desire or compulsion to drink alcohol or use other drugs. In this case, it is suggested that the person attend a meeting or call a sponsor or another member of the program, as soon as possible. In larger urban cities, there are usually several meetings going on in different parts of the city or surrounding suburbs throughout the day.

Once at the meeting, if a member tells the other members about the compulsion and desire to use, most often he or she will not act on it. Other members may share that they, too, have felt that way at times but that it soon passes. The sharing process gives hope and encourages the person to hold on for one more day which reinforces the concept of taking life one day at a time.

The general premise of all the 12-step programs is: Together participants can do what none of them can do alone. For example, in the case of an alcoholic in recovery, the program participant comes to believe that maybe there is some truth to the slogan "we can stay sober; whereas I could never stay sober on my own." In the cases of the compulsive gamblers or the sex addicts in recovery, or whatever the addiction or primary problem, going to meetings drives home the "we" concept and will make the goal of abstaining from destructive behavior patterns obtainable — one day at a time.

One day at a time is a critical concept in all the 12-step programs. We constantly remind each other, depending on the program: "do not pick up a drug, just for today," "do not steal, just for today," "do not give up your boundaries, just for today," etc. Twelve-steppers are encouraged to take it one minute, one hour, one day at a time. The next minute is not promised. Looking ahead to tomorrow, next week, next month, or for the rest of a person's life can be overwhelming. The goal is to surrender some of the burden that presses in when one tries to look at the whole picture. There is a saying among 12-steppers, "If you have one foot on yesterday and one foot on tomorrow, you'll be pissing all over today."

In addition to providing a safe haven, 12-step meetings provide an avenue for meeting people who have found hope and a new way of life; some may even develop into friendships. However, this is not the goal. In time, the newcomer to the program will get to know fellow 12-steppers, if not by name, then by their stories. This is an added benefit of being a part of the program because participants come to know who to go to for help with troublesome issues; this promotes an exchange of sharing. The word "sharing" implies with each other — their experiences, strengths, and hopes which reinforces another 12-step program slogan: "You can only keep what you have by giving it away." Translation: the more the giver gives; the more the giver receives.

More importantly, the more experienced members, or "old-timers," will get to know the newcomer. Recovery is a two-way street: It is the experience of 12-steppers that the more the newcomer lets someone know about him or her, the more help they can receive. As the newcomer opens up, most will find that the suggestions from "old-timers" will seem tailor-made just for them.

Active 12-step members have found meetings to be one of life's most valuable classrooms. While attending the meetings, members learn about the life-changing 12 steps. The steps are to be practically applied to daily living situations; they are a part of the foundation needed for successful living and sustained recovery. The 12 steps and 12 traditions are the foundation of the program. Attending meetings is necessary, but to be "into" the program means to be "into" the steps and traditions. Developing an understanding and working knowledge of the principles represented in the steps and traditions is where lasting effective change happens.

Newcomers will hear and see many things while going to meetings; some things they will agree with; some things not. One can always put what is heard on a mental shelf for later use; surprisingly, many of us discover that something heard during previous meetings helped in problems and situations that arose later.

Most importantly, meetings carry the message to the newcomer that recovery is possible. As people talk about their experience the newcomers relate and begin to believe that they are in the right place to get the kind of help that they need. One meeting at a time, the newcomer's wall of denial is slowly chipped away.

People talk about overcoming their fears, not feeding into the destructive behaviors, being reunited with their families, finally letting go of the past, gaining self-respect, and a myriad of other things. This fuels the hope. Just knowing that others have known a similar kind of despair and feeling of hopelessness brings comfort and strengthens our own desire to get better. Everyone is encouraged to "keep coming back," which is another slogan used in most 12-step programs. The common belief is that "more will be revealed."

We believe that the constant repetition of going to meetings, hearing the simple slogans like "keep coming back, one day at a time," as well as staying in touch with what life was like before the program, creates an atmosphere conducive to sustain recovery.

Most 12-step meetings close with members forming a circle, which is a symbol of the first tradition: "Our common welfare comes first; personal recovery depends on (A.A./NA) unity."

United, most groups recite *The Lord's Prayer* or *The Serenity Prayer* — although some 12-step programs, for example, CoDependents Anonymous have adopted their own prayers.

The Lord's Prayer

Our Father, who art in heaven, hallowed be thy Name.
Thy kingdom come; Thy will be done, on earth as it is in heaven.
Give us this day our daily bread. And forgive us our trespasses,
as we forgive those who trespass against us. And lead us not into temptation,
but deliver us from evil. For Thine is the kingdom, and the power,
and the glory, forever and ever. Amen. (Luke 11:2 KJV)

The Serenity Prayer

God, grant me the serenity to accept the things I cannot change,
the courage to change the things I can, and the wisdom to know the difference.
(St. Francis of Assisi)

Closing Prayer of CoDependents Anonymous*

We thank our Higher Power for all we have received from this meeting.
As we close, may we take with us the wisdom, love, acceptance,
and hope of recovery.

Slogans

Memorizing slogans provides on-the-spot encouragement and helps a 12-stepper to keep life simple. Slogans that many 12-steppers find useful include:

- One day at a time
- We can do what I cannot do alone
- If you do not pick up a drink or drug, you will not use
- First things first
- Easy does it; but do it!
- Let it go
- Progress not perfection
- Turn it over
- Let go and let God
- Relax, God is in charge
- Too much analyzing is paralyzing
- Do not get too Hungry, Angry, Lonely, Tired, or Serious = HALTS
- Honesty, Open-mindedness and Willingness = HOW
- Good Orderly Direction = GOD
- Easing God Out = EGO

---

*Reprinted by permission of CoDA Board of Trustees. From CoDependents Anonymous website. Conference approved 9/31/91.

- False Evidence Appearing Real = FEAR
- Face Everything and Recover = FEAR
- Keep It Simple Stupid = KISS
- Thy will be done, not mine!
- Do not compare yourself out; identify yourself in
- Don't analyze — utilize
- Act as if
- Don't should on yourself
- When I am in my own head, I am in a bad neighborhood
- An addict alone is in bad company
- Take what you want and leave the rest on the shelf for later
- Develop an attitude of gratitude
- You are as sick as your secrets
- Live life on life's terms
- If you have one foot in the past and one foot in the future, you are pissing all over today
- **Today** is the **tomorrow** you worried about **yesterday**
- Feelings are not facts
- Losers do what they want to do; and winners do what they have to do
- This too shall pass
- Don't give up five minutes before the miracle happens!
- Stinking thinking leads to drinking
- Stinking thinking leads to more stinking thinking
- Everything is going to be all right
- On drug dreams: Using drugs is a dream and recovery is a reality
- If you stand around a hot dog stand long enough, you will eventually buy a hot dog
- Stay away from those old people, places, and things
- Just for today

4
Where and When Meetings Are Held

Chapter 12 of this book is a directory of many of the 12-step programs. Each program has a service center headquarters, sometimes called World Service Office or General Service Offices, which handle the administrative duties involved in operating a nonprofit organization. Services provided include information dissemination and literature sales. The list contains mailing addresses, telephone numbers, email, and Internet addresses (if available).

Check your area's telephone directory. Many of the 12-step programs have hotlines that are available 24 hours a day. Members who volunteer to work on the hotline usually have meeting lists and will be able to tell you the location and time of the nearest meeting. Some programs subscribe to answering services or machines that take messages and have someone return the calls.

Printed meeting lists are available at the meetings. Meeting lists can also be requested by mail. To help defray costs, send a self-addressed #10 stamped envelope.

If you have access to a computer that is connected to the Internet, use the URL addresses listed and check out the programs' websites. There is a wealth of information online. Contact by email with questions and requests is another possibility.

As a public service, health sections in major newspapers usually have a calendar of events and sometimes list 12-step meeting times and locations.

5
What is a Home Group?

It is strongly suggested that each member choose, attend, and participate in a home group, a group that feels comfortable, a group that we look forward to being with whenever they meet. This group becomes a "home" to that member when he or she decides to make a commitment to being a part of that group. Having found a "home," the person attends the group meetings regularly, participates in the group conscience *via* business meetings and may even choose to become a "trusted servant" of the group.

There are several other benefits in choosing a home group:

- It allows members an opportunity to get to know other people and lets others get to know them.

- Once a new home group member's attendance is consistent, the other members will look forward to seeing him or her each time the group meets. Also, When a member misses meetings, they usually get a "what's up" call; this simple interaction often prevents a slip.

- The home group is usually where a member takes on his or her first service position. This service may be setting up chairs, making coffee, or serving as secretary of the group. Service to others is an integral part of recovery.

- A home group is also where members participate in regularly scheduled business meetings. During the business meeting, members will vote on issues that affect the group or the fellowship as a whole.

- The home-group members meet, periodically, to take a "group inventory" to determine how well the group is serving it's primary purpose, according to the original 5th Tradition, " . . . to carry the message to the alcoholic who still suffers." This group inventory is also used to determine if the format and atmosphere created in the meeting is effectively serving the newcomer. The newcomer is considered "the most important person at any meeting."

- Members begin to stop isolating as they begin to understand that they are not alone, that they do matter; eventually, they begin to see and believe that people really do care about them.

6
Meeting Formats

Through the process of a group's business meeting, a format is chosen; this is in adherence to the original 4th Tradition that states, "Each A.A. group should be autonomous except in matters affecting other groups or A.A. as a whole." There is usually a legend on the program's meeting list that indicates the format of each group's meeting(s). These formats include, but are not limited to the following.

Open-Discussion Meetings

These meetings are open for attendance by anyone, whether or not that person suffers from the specific problem or addictive behavior. Helping professionals, family members, and supporters are welcomed. It is suggested that as a helping professional you attend at least one open meeting of each program to which you may make a referral. In keeping with the concept of a safe atmosphere of recovery, please introduce yourself as a helping professional and inform participants that your purpose is to observe.

Closed Meetings

These meetings are for members only; exceptions are sometimes made for children but helping professionals that are not members or candidates for membership are excluded.

Speaker Meetings

These meetings have one or two speakers who share their stories and/or experiences since coming into the 12-step program. There is no opening of the meeting for general sharing. Listening only.

Round Robin Meetings

One person shares then selects the next person to share. This selection process continues until the end of the meeting. This approach can be used with any of the other formats, except speaker meetings.

Step-Study Meetings

The program's textbook is used. Members volunteer to read a chapter on one of the 12 steps aloud, in turn. After reading the step, a speaker shares his or her experience in applying that step to everyday life. The meeting is then opened for member participation.

Tradition Study Meetings

This format calls for one of the 12 traditions to be read aloud from the program's textbook. After the reading, a speaker shares his or her experiences with that tradition; then, the meeting is opened for member participation. Members share their experience with the topic tradition. Some groups alternate weekly between the 12 steps and the 12 traditions.

Text Study Meeting

Program-approved pamphlets, other pieces of literature, and chapters from the program's textbook are studied. In some cases, a speaker may share how he or she relates to the literature read; this is followed by group participation. This format is used to familiarize members with the literature and the concept of learning as a group process.

Special-Interest Meetings

These meetings of groups deal with particular issues as they affect a particular recovering population of the 12-step program. The reason for these meetings is to allow more freedom and foster a more comfortable environment in which to share specific experiences. These meetings also offer groups of people specific help in areas outside of their primary problem. Examples include meetings for lawyers, women, men, gay men and women, nurses, and those with AIDS or HIV disease. These special-interest meetings are indicated on the meeting list.

Anniversary/Birthday Celebrations

The groups decide how the celebration format will be handled. Each member has a date that he or she recognizes as the first day of recovery; this date is considered the member's anniversary or birthday and is celebrated annually by the home group. The member celebrating a year (or multiples of years) sometimes chooses the speakers for this special meeting. It is a consensus among 12-steppers that the celebrations are especially important for the newcomer; they show that the program works — that recovery is possible.

How Long Are Meetings?

Most of the meetings last one hour. Some groups have 90-minute meetings and this will be indicated on the meeting list. Ninety-minute meetings are normally reserved for step and tradition study, literature and text study, as well as special-interest group meetings. The extra time allows for reading from the textbook, a speaker, and/or general sharing.

It is suggested that people arrive at meetings 10 or 15 minutes early and stay at least 15 minutes after the meeting ends; this allows for optimum fellowshipping. Experience has shown that the time spent before and after the meetings is where friendships are started and nurtured. People are generally just listening to one another during the meeting. Side conversations are discouraged, as is cross talk. However, it is normal to see people in clusters talking before and after the meeting.

It is also quite common for groups of people to go for a meal or a cup of coffee at nearby restaurants after the meeting; this more casual atmosphere allows people to get to know each other better and has come to be known as "the meeting after the meeting." This quality time, outside of the meeting, promotes more personal in-depth sharing; it is a time to ask questions and get clarification about ideas mentioned at the meeting.

Sometimes, a newcomer can be intimidated by the mere thought of sharing in a meeting with all those people, it may be easier, and a person may feel safer sharing one-on-one. This "meeting after the meeting" is also a good time to get that last bit of encouragement before going back to the daily routine — living life on life's terms.

7
How Often Should Someone Go to Meetings?

This is truly up to the individual. However, it is a good idea, especially in the beginning, to go to a meeting everyday. In fact, it is suggested that newcomers, go to 90 meetings in 90 days; if you're not convinced that this program is for you, then your misery will be refunded. Other suggestions include:

- Go to meetings until you want to go.
- Recovery is a lifetime process.
- Just for today, go to a meeting.
- Come to six meetings before deciding if you want this program.
- Chase these meetings like you chased the drugs/alcohol.
- Go to a meeting when you want to and especially when you don't want to.
- Meeting makers make it.
- Winners do what they have to do; losers do what they want to do.
- More meetings, more recovery. Less meetings, less recovery.

Each of these suggestions can be practically applied one day at a time. The concept of "one day at a time" is not the brain-child of 12-steppers as many of us supposed. In fact, it was Samuel Langhorne Clemens, *aka* Mark Twain, who wrote, "The best thing about life is that it comes at me one day at a time."

How often a person goes to meetings also depends on the availability of meetings in a specific area. In metropolitan communities, most 12-step programs have meetings available around-the-clock, everyday of the week; however, 12-step meetings may not be that plentiful in small cities and towns. In some cases, there may be no meetings available in the immediate area; this might mean that the nearest meeting is a considerable drive away. However, if someone really wants help, nothing will deter him or her from getting to a meeting.

As a testament to this fact, a Canadian friend of mine lived over 250 miles from the nearest meeting. She would save money, take a day off work, ride the train, and stay in a motel just to attend the meeting. So, there is no plausible excuse for not getting to a meeting.

If a person is unemployed, it is suggested that, especially in the beginning, he or she go to more than one meeting per day. This is suggested because it is unwise to be alone for too long, especially during this most vulnerable period and too much idle time may threaten one's ability to stay focused on the program. There is much wisdom in the 12-step adage: "An addict alone is in bad company."

If no public transportation is available, most program members are amenable to providing rides to and from the meetings. Another option would be to call the program's area hotline and let them know that a ride is needed. Usually, if a member can get to a meeting, a ride back home is not a problem. Newcomers should be encouraged to get the telephone numbers of people attending the meeting; these numbers promote interaction and can also lead to rides to and from the meetings.

8
How Long Should
Someone Go to Meetings?

Members go to meetings *one day at a time* for as long as it takes. It is understood in the programs that recovery is a lifetime process; however, it is not quite so overwhelming to look at something that needs to be done just one day at a time. A newcomer should not try to determine or make a decision as to how long he or she will have to go to meetings.

In time, new members usually discover that they *like* to go to meetings especially when they start to see the rewards and begin to realize the beauty of not having to handle life alone. Some members have even found that their joys are doubled and their burdens are halved as they share their experiences with other people.

Step 2 mentions that we "came to believe that a power greater than ourselves could restore us to sanity." How long this "coming to believe" or restoration process will take varies — " . . . sometimes slowly, sometimes quickly . . . but it will always come if we are willing to work for it." (*Alcoholics Anonymous* 1976).

Fitting 12-Step Meetings into a Busy Schedule

It is suggested that schedules be planned around the 12-step meetings because without recovery, everything else just falls apart. We hope that a person will not have to learn the hard way that without the help of regular meetings there might come a time when there is no schedule to plan or plans to schedule.

The programs are comprised of people from all walks of life including physicians, law students, housewives, and single parents with several children that go to meetings regularly — some even daily. These people balance their days between work, school, errands, cooking meals, and studying and still are able to make meetings regularly. Some 12-steppers have to travel in their work — one day in Seattle, two days in New York — so when they reach their destination they call the hotline, find out where the meetings are, and get there.

If a person is serious about recovery, they will be serious about getting to meetings; after all, it is life and well-being that is at stake. We may not be responsible for what ails us, but we are responsible for our own recovery.

Taking the time to attend a meeting can make a busy schedule go more smoothly. The tasks and feelings of the day seem less overwhelming. Meetings can provide a source of spiritual refreshment, renewal, and encouragement to go forward with whatever is at hand. Just going into the meeting room and seeing other people struggling to recover can have a positive impact on a person's attitude toward the rest of the day.

Before, after, and sometimes during the meeting hugs flow freely. (There are a lot of huggers in most of the 12-step programs.) On some days, a hug is all that a person needs. Or perhaps a smile from the across the room will give someone just the enthusiasm, courage, and serenity needed to make it one more day. Most 12-steppers find this to be true, if they just "keep coming back" to meetings.

What Is the Money in the Basket Used For?

The 7th Tradition states that each group " . . . ought to be fully self-supporting declining outside contributions." During the secretary's report of fellowship-related announcements, a basket for donations is passed. Funds collected are used to help maintain the group; it is strictly a personal choice whether to give or not to give. The monies cover expenses such as rent of the meeting space, literature, key tags, or "chips" denoting months and years successfully on the program, and refreshments. The groups usually choose to donate a portion of the money to the program's area service committee. Most of the program-approved pamphlets available at the meetings are free; however, textbooks and program magazines are usually sold at cost.

Some institutions seek to donate the meeting space; they note that having the meetings in their facility is doing them a favor by providing a service to their clients, however, because of the 7th Tradition, the group must pay rent. This tradition also protects the group from outside influences. By accepting donations, the group would be opening itself to these benefactors possibly trying to influence the flavor and purpose of the group. In addition, this tradition can be practically applied to members' personal lives. Members are encouraged to learn to assume responsibility for life by being self-supporting.

Secretary's Report

The secretary's report includes announcements of upcoming service, social, and fellowship events. Members' anniversary/birthday celebration dates and locations are also announced. Chips or key tags are given to signify months and years in the program.

Although some people may be tempted to leave for a break during this portion of the meeting, it is better to stay. It is supportive and inspirational to see the other members receive their chips and key tags. This is especially true for the presentation of the chip signifying "24 hours or less or just a desire for a new way of life."

12-Step Conventions

Conventions are usually planned and organized by service committees of the 12-step programs. Conventions are regional gatherings that provide an atmosphere of recovery, fellowship, and fun. They are usually a weekend filled with topical workshops, speaker meetings, and social activities of the 12-step program.

Service committees host conventions, primarily to carry the message to newcomers that recovery is possible. Since profit is not the goal of conventions, they are usually very affordable. The costs involved are transportation, hotel accommodations (lower convention rates are usually available), food, and a nominal convention registration fee which offsets the cost of hosting the convention.

Thanks to donations by fellow members and fund-raising events hosted by the convention committee, newcomers, including those in treatment facilities who are financially unable to attend any other way, are made welcome because indigent registration packages are usually available. Check with the convention committee hosting the convention.

Speaker meetings and workshop topics include sponsorship, newcomers, welcome to recovery, steps, and dealing with illness in recovery. Marathon meetings are non-stop meetings held during the entire convention. Social and entertainment activities usually scheduled include golf tournaments, comic shows, dances, pool parties, talent shows, excursion tours, as well as activities for the children.

Loner Groups

Some of the 12-step programs have an outreach component for people that, for whatever reason, cannot physically get to meetings. Within the 12-step program of Narcotics Anonymous this component is referred to as the "loner group." While the application within the different 12-step programs may differ, the goal is still the same. These loner groups seek to reach isolated people with the message that recovery is possible regardless of a person's inability to attend meetings. Even if a particular 12-step program does not have a loner group, there is a possibility that, if the demand proves great enough, such a group can be initiated.

Most of the 12-step programs have publications that are mailed monthly to members who request to be placed on the loner mailing list. Regular members are also encouraged to participate. The publications have recovery-related articles along with letters from loners. Members who receive the publication often write to each other which promotes recovery.

For example, a letter from a new member of a loner group may request assistance in learning more about the 12 steps and how to practically apply them to daily life. A member experienced in the 12 steps will respond by writing. Once this initial contact is made, it is often followed up with telephone interaction. Frequent exchange of information from the non-loner, who does have the benefit of attending meetings, to the loner is common. This process becomes a "meeting," even though it is by mail.

With today's technology, there are more ways than ever for the loners to connect with the 12-step program and its members; email and Internet access is a growing mode of communication. Chat rooms are available on the web for 12-steppers. While some are not official program chat room sites, they can provide 24-hour availability. Query a search engine, like Yahoo, and enter the words, "chat rooms, recovery" several links to websites will come up.

Some of the 12-step programs' annual international conventions include loner group meetings. At these meetings, loners get the opportunity to meet the members they have been corresponding with, a most gratifying experience indeed.

9
Starting a 12-Step Group

If you are interested in starting a new group, contact the program's headquarters first. All headquarters provide information on how to start groups. Some programs have starter kits available that include valuable information about the program, suggestions on meeting formats, group registration forms, and order forms for program literature. Following these suggestions will enable the group to effectively carry the recovery message of that particular program.

Community organizations, hospitals, treatment centers, counseling centers, detoxification units, DWI facilities, prisons, and other institutions that would like to have a 12-step meeting started in their facilities should understand that in order to be a legitimate and sanctioned group, it must be open to the general public. This is in keeping with the 12th Tradition which states, "Anonymity is the spiritual foundation of all of our Traditions, ever reminding us to place principles before personalities." (*Alcoholics Anonymous* 1976).

Therefore, anonymity is of utmost importance, which includes not being under any kind of surveillance, etc. If these conditions are not possible, then seek to have what is generally known as a "H&I" (Hospital and Institution) meeting brought into the facility. Contact headquarters for the nearest Area Service H&I Committee. This committee would be responsible for sending a panel of members into the facility to carry the message of that particular program. The facility would set up the criteria for admittance. This type of meeting is attended only by the facilities' population and the 12-step program's panels. Treatment centers, prisons, halfway houses, hospitals, and mental-health clinics are the kinds of institutions that are usually interested in this type of meeting structure.

Other viable resources for start-up groups and/or meetings include:

- Contacting someone you may already know that is a member of a 12-step program. Ask him or her for help. They may already have experience or know of someone experienced in starting meetings that would welcome the opportunity to start a new meeting. Usually when someone agrees to help, they are willing to make a commitment to attend on a regular basis, at least until attendance is consistent and trusted servants, voted in through a group conscience, are in place.

- Existing groups are open to sponsoring meetings in other facilities; this is often a group's way of carrying the message of recovery into the community.

12-Step Meetings in Hospitals and Institutions

Meetings in hospitals and institutions are especially good for those suffering. Seeds of a new way of life are planted. If the person is incarcerated, then it is likely that his or her lifestyle, habits, or behavior had something to do with the problem. This period of incarceration may be a "bottom" for the person. More often than not, it takes a person reaching an emotional, physical, and spiritual bottom before realizing there is a problem and that help is needed. While you have their attention, plant all the seeds you can. Though we cannot make the seeds grow, it is our responsibility as fellow human beings to plant some seeds.

As discussed earlier, the 12-step programs have committees especially formed to serve hospitals and institutions. Contact headquarters or local hotlines to request that a meeting be started in your facility. The committee will provide experienced program members who, in most cases, have been trained to take meetings into hospitals and institutions. These panels of recovery people will come to your facility on a regular and consistent basis to bring the message of recovery to your patients.

What Is Needed to Start a 12-Step Meeting?

- Meeting room space should be secured and reserved for a specific day and time. Once the day and time are chosen, it is extremely important that the meetings take place every week at that same time and location.
- A supply of approved pamphlets and other literature of the 12-step program.
- Individuals to make sure that the meeting room is open and set up appropriately.
- The meeting space will be needed for 60 - 90 minutes, depending on the chosen meeting format; this allows time for room set-up, breakdown, and cleanup.

Other Factors to Consider

It is of utmost importance that the meeting day, time, and location be kept consistent each week. Please keep this in mind when seeking a location. Access should be available every time the group is scheduled to meet. Once the meeting is listed in the area's meeting list, anyone coming to that building on that particular day and time should find a meeting. If the meeting day should fall on a holiday, it is especially important that the meeting takes place. Holidays are normally very stressful for people in early recovery. If a meeting must be canceled, let the hotline committee know, so that changes can be announced throughout the 12-step community during the secretary's report, and visibly post the nearest alternative meeting location.

To better understand the importance of consistency, consider this scenario — a 12-stepper has an overwhelming urge to drink or drug and desperately needs a meeting to get through the crisis. He or she looks at the meeting list, finds a meeting, and gets there only to find that the doors are locked, that the meeting is canceled. What does that person do? He or she might easily choose to use. So, following the suggestions regarding cancellations is very important. If the nearest available meeting time and place is posted on the door, a life could be saved, a recovery sustained.

It is just one person. But in the 12-step community, that lone individual looking for help is of the utmost importance because that person might be me.

Understand, too, that all it takes is two people to have a meeting. Once the program's opening statements are read or one of the members says, "The meeting is now open," the meeting is in progress whether there are 50 people or two people in attendance.

What Can Be Expected When Starting New Meetings?

When starting a new meeting, expect poor attendance. Word has to spread that there is a new meeting available. For example, a member of a 12-step program in a mid-western state started a new meeting; he was the only person at the meeting every week for about a month. This meeting was also the first meeting in this particular town, so the odds were really against him. However, he did not give up. He wrote a letter asking for members' experiences in similar situations that was printed in the program's magazine. A member read his plea for help and responded. The member encouraged him not to give up five minutes before the miracle happened. Well, during week five, a miracle happened: five people showed up for the meeting — it has been growing strong ever since.

Finding Out More About the 12-Step Program

It is suggested that anyone interested in getting first-hand information on a particular 12-step meeting sit in on an open meeting. Check with headquarters or the local hotline for an open meeting in your area. Everyone is welcome at an open meeting. See Chapter 6 for more about meeting formats.

Please respect the anonymity of the program's members. It is a good idea to introduce yourself as a professional, family member, supporter, or curious spectator and state your purpose for attending.

It is a good idea to order and read a copy of the program's textbook and other literature. The literature contains information on working the steps, traditions, sponsorship, and members' stories. The literature gives insight into the problem being addressed by a particular program.

10
Sponsorship

What Is a Sponsor?

A sponsor is a more experienced member of the program who guides the newcomer through the process of recovery. Generally, a sponsor has at least one year or more in the program. However, some cities have so many new people coming into the 12-step programs, so fast, that supply and demand makes such criteria unrealistic. With this in mind, some 12-step communities suggest a sponsor have six months living the program. The most effective sponsors have:

- A working knowledge of the 12 Steps and 12 Traditions
- Personal experience dealing with life in recovery
- A willingness to listen
- A willingness to help another person build a foundation for recovery by sharing their experience, strength, and hope
- A willingness to guide a person through the 12-steps based on their own personal experience
- A willingness to make suggestions and refrain from giving advice

The 12-step programs are based on the therapeutic value of people who share a common problem helping each other. Therefore, having a sponsor provides the opportunity to learn to trust and be trusted, perhaps for the first time. Many of us wrestle with our problems alone for so long there is a tendency to isolate. Even after coming into recovery we have to come to believe that we are not alone and that we never have to be alone again. We can do together what I could not do alone.

A sponsor is someone to contact when we need someone to talk to or feel unsure about decisions that have to be made. A sponsor also helps with problems and questions not only when times are tough but also during the good times.

Other good examples of when to call a sponsor would be when something triggers a member to think about using, or when unpleasant memories surface during the night that, in the past, caused a member to get drunk or high. Calling a sponsor usually provides comfort, identification of the feelings, and hope that, in spite of how the person feels, he or she does not have to self-destruct.

A sponsor provides a listening ear and acts as a sounding board for decisions that have to be made. Most 12-step programs suggest that all major decisions be talked over with a sponsor. The sponsor does not make that decision. The sponsor shares his or her experiences as they relate to the decision. If a sponsor has no experience in a particular area, a wise sponsor will direct the person to someone else who has had appropriate experience. Guidance is freely given so that the person gets practice in making sound decisions.

Sponsors make suggestions, based on their experiences, strengths, and hopes. Sponsors who have had experience with a particular situation that is presented, will share with the person what their feelings were and how they handled a similar situation using the tools of recovery. This shared-experience process keeps the newcomer from feeling alone with their problem. In the fullness of time, the newcomer sheds the question that haunts most of our lives, "Am I the only one in the world who feels like this?" The realization that we are not so different, not alone in our problems, gives us therapeutic relief.

It is the member's choice whether to take the suggestions once they are given. There are no "musts" in any of the 12-step programs. Sponsorship is an effective tool of recovery because sponsors are people who have suffered with the same problem or addiction and are on the same road seeking recovery from the chains that once bound them. Sponsors understand because they have been there.

Good news, victories, and hopes are also shared with a sponsor. Some of the principles, both the sponsor and the person being sponsored practice when developing this crucial relationship are unconditional love, selfless giving, patience, tolerance, honesty with another human being, and trust.

A sponsor is neither a counselor nor a mental-health professional. If the sponsor is a counselor professionally, that role is left at the door of the 12-step program. The sponsor is in recovery, too. Sponsors are equals who are members of the program also on the road in search of lasting recovery. When additional help is needed, members are encouraged to seek professional guidance. Doctors, accountants, marriage counselors, and financial brokers should all be found outside of the program.

Sponsors are not to be used as therapists, loan companies, or landlords, nor do they work the program for you. They listen, share their experience, and guide the people they sponsor through the 12 steps and 12 traditions.

In 12-step circles, it is suggested that a sponsor should be of the same gender. The newcomer to the program is quite vulnerable. For some of us, this is the first time we have expressed our true feelings, our secrets, and our fears.

Experience has shown that this new relationship with a member of the opposite gender could be misinterpreted, which if acted upon, could reduce the chances for sustained recovery for both parties.

One of the advantages of choosing a same-gender sponsor is that the member will get to know more about himself or herself as a member of that gender. Experience has also shown that it is sometimes more difficult for a male to talk to a female and *vice versa*. As open dialogue is of paramount importance in the sponsor/newcomer relationship, it makes good sense to avoid gender-based communication problems. In addition:

- A sponsor is an objective person on the outside looking in.
- Sponsors are able to see patterns that emerge and point out problem areas before the person sponsored gets into more trouble.
- Sponsors see how much a person has changed and offers encouragement along the way. There's a 12-step program slogan that defines the need for a sponsor, "Other people see you better than you see yourself."
- Sponsors generally stress accountability.
- Sponsors help the people they sponsor stay focused on recovery.

Sponsorship is a two-way street, it is a relationship built to help the sponsor and the person being sponsored. Therefore, people who opt not to choose a sponsor, or later not to sponsor others, are cheating themselves and fellow human beings out of a great opportunity to grow spiritually and emotionally.

Sponsorship is a vital tool of recovery. Sponsorship allows another person in so that together they can begin the process of healing and learning how to live one day at a time.

Sponsorship is a beacon in the night. This is especially true in the beginning, when the new member feels that his or her whole life is one open festering wound. Newcomers usually say they feel like they are bombarded by an onslaught of emotions, feelings, and painful memories. They doubt that the program can and will work for them; and they are usually angry because of their failure to control their own lives.

Newcomers normally have a myriad of complex problems that are a direct result of an out-of-control lifestyle. These problems will not go away overnight and will take time and patience to remedy — patience that newcomers usually do not possess. This is where a sponsor can shed a bit of light by sharing with the newcomer his or her own experiences, strengths, and hopes. Sponsors can empathize because they have been where the newcomer is. They have known the hopelessness, desperation, humiliation, and powerlessness to control or change themselves for the better. Someone was there for us when we first sought help in the program; so, we want to be available for the newcomer. The program is built on this mutual sharing of recovery. We strongly believe our unofficial motto: "You cannot keep what you have unless you give it away."

Choosing a Sponsor

Once people get into the habit of going to meetings, they will soon meet a person they may consider asking to be their sponsor. The newcomer needs to ask that person: "Will you be my sponsor?" It is just that simple.

"Suppose they say no?" the newcomer might ask. Usually, 12-steppers say, "yes." It is an honor to be asked. Still, valid reasons exist to say, "no." There is a possibility the person already sponsors all the people he or she can effectively deal with. The person also may not have enough time in the program; or the person may even need to check with his or her sponsor first before committing to sponsorship. So, if a potential sponsor says "no," the newcomer is encouraged to ask someone else. It is all a part of the recovery process, learning how to deal with rejection and not letting that stop you from reaching out for help. If one person says "no" it just means that there is someone else waiting to say "yes!"

Should a Person Have More Than One Sponsor?

Among 12-steppers, it is strongly suggested that a newcomer have only one sponsor, this cuts down on the confusion and the tendency to play one sponsor against the other. With more than one sponsor a person tends to give bits and pieces of their history and their feelings to each one, but a single sponsor is told the whole story. It is more of a stretch to have one sponsor. When a person comes into the program, it is time to take off the masks. The more in-depth the sponsor gets to know the new member, the more individualized help the newcomer receives.

How Does Someone Develop a Relationship With a Sponsor?

A relationship usually begins with the telephone, one of the most valuable tools of recovery. Even if the new member is unsure of what to say, it's strongly suggested to call and just say "hello." The sponsor will usually take it from there and initiate a conversation. Sponsors are familiar with the difficulty the newcomer finds in making these calls. They know because, remember, they were newcomers at one time themselves. The newcomer just has to have the willingness to initiate the call. The newcomer will find it gets easier as he or she matures in the program. In time, a new and positive habit, talking things over with a sponsor, is developed.

It is good to meet your sponsor at a meeting. This allows time to talk before and after the meeting, which is both convenient and a comfort. Many people opt to go for coffee or tea with their sponsors after the meeting.

How Often Is a Sponsor Contacted?

The frequency of the calls to the sponsor is up to the individual. In some cases, sponsors suggest that especially in the beginning, new members call every day. The answer depends on the sponsor's individual style and, in some cases, how he or she has been sponsored. A simple talk with a sponsor can provide the guidance and encouragement a person needs to continue with the tasks of the day and keep the newcomer focused on the goal of lasting recovery.

11
Suggestions for the Helping Professional

- Sit in on open-discussion meetings. Identify yourself as a professional to protect the anonymity of the members of the group. Contact the 12-step program to find out the location of an "open" meeting. (See Chapter 6, Meeting Formats for further explanation.)

- Obtain and keep copies of the latest list of 12-step program meetings in your area.

- Keep copies of the most current edition of *12-Step Programs: A Resource Guide for Helping Professionals* at your office and at home for those after-hour cries for help.

- Ask to see the "clean and sober" key tags. These key tags, plastic and metal coins, represent length of abstinence, i.e., 24 hours, 30 days, 60 days, 90 days, six months, nine months, one year, 18-months, and multiples of years. However, respect your clients anonymity and do not insist that you see it.

- Purchase a supply of 12-step program literature — including a few textbooks.

- Have members of the 12-step program start meetings in your facility and invite your clients to attend. These meetings are great exposure to the hope offered in these programs. A seed is planted — **recovery is possible.** (See Chapter 9 for more options.)

Handout for the Client: What Can I Do?

- Do not pick up (a drink or drug) and you will not use — **just for today.**

- Maybe you want to take a drink or drug (that is normal); but remember you do not have to act on that feeling. Feelings are not facts.

- Tell somebody who is consciously staying away from a drink or a drug how you feel; usually, if you talk about it, you will not use. Call the hotline of a 12-step program like Alcoholics Anonymous (A.A.), Narcotics Anonymous (NA), or Cocaine Anonymous (CA). Get to the meeting as soon as possible. You cannot stay clean and sober alone.

- Once at the meeting, raise your hand and let the others know that you are new in recovery and that you want help.

- After the meeting, do not run out. Stay to get the help you need. If you are afraid to ask during the meeting, ask for help before you leave the premises. People in recovery want to help you as others helped them. They have been exactly where you are at some time or another.

- Get members' telephone numbers and call, before you drink or drug.

- Free literature is available at meetings. Get it and read it. Purchase the program's book and read it.

- Watch the people who raise their hands as having a year or more clean and sober and ask one of them to be your sponsor. It is not etched in stone that you keep that sponsor. After you have been clean and sober for a while, you can always change sponsors. The point being you need someone now. Do not wait for the "perfect" time to find the "perfect" sponsor.

- There is no such thing as the "perfect" time nor is there a "perfect" sponsor. It is suggested that males sponsor males and females sponsor females.

- Stay away from slippery people, places, and things — family included.

- If someone asks you to take a drink or to get high, do not stop to chat, move on. Do not explain — "friends don't need an explanation and enemies will not believe you anyway."

- If someone insists that you take a drink or a drug, simply say, "I'm allergic" and remove yourself. People do not want to see someone have an allergic reaction.

- Remember you may not be responsible for your disease, but you are responsible for your recovery.

- Find a Higher Power and pray. It is said by 12-steppers that, "There will come a time where the only thing between you and self-destruction is your Higher Power."

- Relapse is not a prerequisite of any 12-step program.

12
Directory of Programs

Adult Children Anonymous (ACA)
World Service Office
P.O. Box 35623
Los Angeles, CA 90035
Fax: (213) 651-1710
Ottawa Canada ACA Group: http://www.ncf.carleton.ca/acainnerpeace

Summary

A 12-step program whose members are people from families with a history of physical, emotional, and/or verbal abuse, workaholism, drug or alcohol addictions, incest, etc.

Goal*

ACA is a support group or self-help fellowship with one purpose: To heal ourselves and to carry our message of hope to other ACA's who are still suffering.

Requirement for Membership

A desire for spiritual growth and recovery from unhealthy behavior.

---

*Reprinted with permission from Adult Children Anonymous Ottawa Group's website.

Adult Children of Alcoholics Anonymous (ACA)*
ACA World Service Organization, Inc.
P.O. Box 3216
Torrance, CA 90510
Telephone: (310) 534-1815
Email: info@adultchildren.org
Email for literature: mailto:literature@adultchildren.org
World Service Organization Website: http://www.adultchildren.org/

Summary*

Adult Children of Alcoholics is a 12-steps, 12-traditions program of women and men who grew up in alcoholic or otherwise dysfunctional homes. We meet with each other in a mutually respectful, safe environment and acknowledge our common experiences. We discover how childhood affected us in the past and influences us in the present problem. We take positive action. By practicing the 12 steps, focusing on The Solution, and accepting a loving Higher Power of our understanding, we find freedom from the past and a way to improve our lives today.

Alcoholics Anonymous (A.A.)
World Service, Inc.
P.O. Box 459, Grand Central Station
New York, NY 10163
Telephone: (212) 870-3400
Website: http://www.alcoholics-anonymous.org

Summary

A fellowship of people of all ages who are or suspect that they may have a drinking problem and want to do something about it.

Goal

To stop drinking, maintain sobriety, and learn how to live a full and purposeful life.

3rd Tradition

The only requirement for membership is a desire to stop drinking.

Self-Assessment Questions*

1. Have you decided to stop drinking for a week or so, but only lasted for a couple days?

    (Most of us in A.A. made all kinds of promises to ourselves and to our families. We could not keep them. Then we came to A.A. A.A. said: "Just try not to drink today." If you do not drink today, you cannot get drunk today.)

2. Do you wish people would mind their own business about your drinking — stop telling you what to do?

    (In A.A. we do not tell anyone to do anything. We just talk about our own drinking, the trouble we got into, and how we stopped. We will be glad to help you, if you want us to.)

3. Have you ever switched from one kind of drink to another in hope that this would keep you from getting drunk?

---

*Reprinted with permission of A.A. World Services, Inc. from *A.A. General Service Conference-approved Literature*. © 1973 A.A. World Services, Inc. The Twelve Steps, Twelve 12 Traditions, and brief excerpts are reprinted with permission of Alcoholics Anonymous World Services, Inc. Permission to reprint this material does not mean that A.A. has reviewed or approved the contents of this publication, nor that A.A. agrees with the views expressed herein. A.A. is a program of recovery from alcoholism only — use of these excerpts in connection with programs and activities which are patterned after A.A., but which address other problems, or in any other non-A.A. context, does not imply otherwise.

(We tried all kinds of ways. We made our drinks weak. Or just drank beer. Or we did not drink cocktails. Or only drank on weekends. You name it, we tried it. But if we drank anything with alcohol in it, we usually got drunk eventually.)

4. Have you had to have an eye-opener upon awakening during the past year?

    (Do you need a drink to get started or to stop shaking? This is a pretty sure sign that you are not drinking "socially.")

5. Do you envy people who can drink without getting into trouble?

    (At one time or another, most of us have wondered why we were not like most people, who really can take it or leave it.)

6. Have you had problems connected with drinking during the past year?

    (Be honest. Doctors say that if you have a problem with alcohol and keep on drinking, it will get worse — never better. Eventually, you will die, or end up in an institution for the rest of your life. The only hope is to stop drinking.)

7. Has your drinking caused trouble at home?

    (Before we came into A.A., most of us said that it was the people or problems at home that made us drink. We could not see that our drinking just made everything worse. It never solved problems anywhere or anytime.)

8. Do you ever try to get "extra" drinks at a party because you do not get enough?

    (Most of us used to have a "few" before we started out if we thought it was going to be that kind of party. And if drinks were not served fast enough, we would go some place else to get more.)

9. Do you tell yourself you can stop drinking any time you want to, even though you keep getting drunk when you don't mean to?

    (Many of us kidded ourselves into thinking that we drank because we wanted to. After we came into A.A., we found that once we started to drink, we couldn't stop.)

10. Have you missed days of work or school because of drinking?

    (Many of us admit now that we "called in sick" lots of times when the truth was that we were hung-over or on a drunk.)

11. Do you have "blackouts"?

    (A "blackout" is when we have been drinking for hours or days that we cannot remember. When we came to A.A., we found out that this is a pretty sure sign of alcoholic drinking.)

12. Have you ever felt that your life would be better if you did not drink?

(Many of us started to drink because drinking made life seem better, at least for a while. By the time we got into A.A., we felt trapped. We were drinking to live and living to drink. We were sick and tired of being sick and tired.)

Did you answer yes four or more times? If so, you are probably in trouble with alcohol. Why do we say this? Thousands of people in A.A. have said so for many years. They found out the truth about themselves — the hard way.

But again, only you can decide whether you think A.A. is for you. Try to keep an open mind on the subject. If the answer is yes, we will be glad to show you how we stopped drinking ourselves. Just call.

A.A. does not promise to solve your life's problems. But we can show you how we are learning to live without drinking "one day at a time." We stay away from that "first drink." If there is no first one, there cannot be a tenth one. And when we got rid of alcohol, we found that life became much more manageable.

Alcoholics Anonymous and AIDS (Type of A.A. Group)
Alcoholics Anonymous
World Service, Inc.
P.O. Box 459, Grand Central Station
New York, NY 10163
Telephone: (212) 870-3400
Website: http://www.alcoholics-anonymous.org

Summary

A special-interest meeting group for members of A.A. who also have AIDS or HIV disease.

Goal

To stop drinking, remain sober, and learn how to live a full and purposeful life.

Al-Anon Family Group Headquarters, Inc. (Al-Anon)
1600 Corporate Landing Parkway
Virginia Beach, Va. 23454-5617
Telephone: 757-563-1600 or 1-888-356-9996
Fax: 757-563-1655
Website: http://www.al-anon.alateen.org

Summary

A program for relatives and friends who are or were affected by contact with a problem drinker.

Suggested Al-Anon Preamble to the 12 Steps*

The Al-Anon Family Groups are a fellowship of relatives and friends of alcoholics who share their experience, strength, and hope in order to solve their common problems. We believe alcoholism is a family illness and that changed attitudes can aid recovery.

Al-Anon is not allied with any sect, denomination, political entity, organization, or institution; does not engage in any controversy; neither endorses nor opposes any cause. There are no dues for membership. Al-Anon is self-supporting through its own voluntary contributions.

Al-Anon has but one purpose: to help families of alcoholics. We do this by practicing the 12 steps, by welcoming and giving comfort to families of alcoholics, and by giving understanding and encouragement to the alcoholic.

Self-Assessment Questions —
Are You Troubled by Someone's Drinking?**

Millions of people are affected by the excessive drinking of someone close. The following questions are designed to help you decide whether or not you need Al-Anon.

1. Do you worry about how much someone drinks?

2. Do you have money problems because of someone else's drinking?

3. Do you tell lies to cover up for some one else's drinking?

4. Do you feel that if the drinker loved you, he or she would stop drinking to please you?

---

*Reprinted with permission of Al-Anon Family Group Headquarters, Inc. from *Suggested Al-Anon Preamble to the Twelve Steps.* ©1973 by Al-Anon Family Group Headquarters, Inc.
**Reprinted with permission of Al-Anon Family Group Headquarters, Inc. from *Are You Troubled by Someone's Drinking?* © 1980 by Al-Anon Family Group Headquarters. Inc.

5. Do you blame the drinker's behavior on his or her companions?

6. Are plans frequently upset or canceled or meals delayed because of the drinker?

7. Do you make threats, such as, "If you don't stop drinking, I'll leave you"?

8. Do you secretly try to smell the drinker's breath?

9. Are you afraid to upset someone for fear it will set off a drinking bout?

10. Have you been hurt or embarrassed by a drinker's behavior?

11. Are holidays and gatherings spoiled because of drinking?

12. Have you considered calling the police for help in fear of abuse?

13. Do you search for hidden alcohol?

14. Do you often ride in a car with a driver who has been drinking?

15. Have you refused social invitations out of fear or anxiety?

16. Do you sometimes feel like a failure when you think of the lengths you have gone to control the drinker?

17. Do you think that if the drinker stopped drinking, your other problems would be solved?

18. Do you ever threaten to hurt yourself to scare the drinker?

19. Do you feel angry, confused, or depressed most of the time?

20. Do you feel there is no one who understands your problems?

If you have answered yes to three or more of these questions, Al-Anon or Alateen may be able to help. You can contact Al-Anon or Alateen by looking in your local telephone directory or by writing to Al-Anon Family Group Headquarters, Inc.

Alateen
Al-Anon Family Group Headquarters, Inc.
1600 Corporate Landing Parkway
Virginia Beach, VA 23454-5617
(757) 563-1600
For meeting information: 1-888-4AL-ANON or 1-888-425-2666
Fax: 757-563-1655
Email: wso@al-anon.org
Website: http://www.al-anon.alateen.org

Summary*

Alateen is a fellowship of young Al-Anon members, usually teen-agers, whose lives have been affected by someone's else's drinking. The only requirement for membership is to have a problem of alcoholism in a relative or friend.

Young people come together to:

- Share experience, strength, and hope with each other
- Discuss their difficulties
- Learn effective ways to cope with their problems
- Encourage one another
- Help each other understand the principles of the Al-Anon program

Alateen members learn:

- Compulsive drinking is a disease
- They can detach themselves emotionally from the drinker's problems while continuing to love the person
- They are not the cause of anyone else's drinking or behavior
- They cannot change or control anyone but themselves
- They have spiritual and intellectual resources with which to develop their own potentials, no matter what happens at home
- They can build satisfying and rewarding life experiences for themselves
- Alateen members meet in church halls, school rooms, or other suitable places (many times in the same building as an Al-Anon group, but in a separate room).

---

*Reprinted with permission of the Al-Anon Family Group Headquarters, Inc. from *Facts About Alateen.* ©1969 by Al-Anon Family Group Headquarters, Inc.

Self-Assessment Questions —
Is Someone's Drinking Getting to You?*

Is someone's drinking getting to you? Alateen is for you. Alateen is for young people whose lives have been affected by someone else's drinking. The following 20 questions are to help you decide whether or not Alateen is for you.

1. Do you have a parent, close friend, or relative whose drinking upsets you?

2. Do you cover up your real feelings by pretending you don't care?

3. Are holidays and gatherings spoiled because of drinking?

4. Do you tell lies to cover up for someone else's drinking or what's happening in your home?

5. Do you stay out of the house as much as possible because you hate it there?

6. Are you afraid to upset someone for fear it will set off a drinking bout?

7. Do you feel nobody really loves you or cares what happens to you?

8. Are you afraid or embarrassed to bring your friends home?

9. Do you think the drinker's behavior is caused by you, other members of your family, friends, or rotten breaks in life?

10. Do you make threats such as, "If you don't stop drinking, fighting, I'll run away"?

11. Do you make promises about behavior, such as, "I'll get better school marks, go to church, or keep my room clean" in exchange for a promise that the drinking and fighting stop?

12. Do you feel that if your mom or dad loved you, she or he would stop drinking?

13. Do you ever threaten or actually hurt yourself to scare your parents into saying, "I'm sorry," or "I love you"?

14. Do you believe no one could possibly understand how you feel?

15. Do you have money problems because of someone else's drinking?

16. Are mealtimes frequently delayed because of the drinker?

17. Have you considered calling the police because of the drinker's abusive behavior?

18. Have you refused dates out of fear or anxiety?

19. Do you think your problems would be solved if the drinking stopped?

---

*Reprinted with permission of Al-Anon Family Group Headquarters, Inc. from *Is Someone's Drinking Getting to You?* ©1981 by Al-Anon Family Group Headquarters, Inc.

20. Do you ever treat people (teachers, schoolmates, teammates, etc.) unjustly because you are angry at someone else for drinking too much?

If you have answered yes to some of these questions, Alateen may help you. You can contact Al-Anon or Alateen by looking in your local telephone directory or by writing to Al-Anon Family Group Headquarters, Inc.

Alatot
Al-Anon Family Group Headquarters, Inc.
1600 Corporate Landing Parkway
Virginia Beach, VA 23454-5617
(757) 563-1600
For meeting information: 1-888-4AL-ANON or 1-888-425-2666
Fax: 757-563-1655
Email: wso@al-anon.org
Website: http://www.al-anon.alateen.org

Summary*

Alatot is a fellowship of young Al-Anon members, usually children, whose lives have been affected by someone's else's drinking. The only requirement for membership is to have a problem of alcoholism in a relative or friend. Adult members of Al-Anon Family Groups facilitate these group meetings.

*Reprinted with permission of Al-Anon Family Group Headquarters, Inc. ©1984 by Al-Anon Family Group Headquarters, Inc.

Adult Children of Alcoholics
Al-Anon Family Group Headquarters, Inc.
1600 Corporate Landing Parkway
Virginia Beach, VA 23454-5617
(757) 563-1600
For meeting information: 1-888-4AL-ANON or 1-888-425-2666
Fax: 757-563-1655
Email: wso@al-anon.org
Website: http://www.al-anon.alateen.org

Summary

A special-interest group made up of adult Al-Anon members who have grown up with an alcoholic as a parent or guardian.

Self-Assessment Questions*

Al-Anon is for families, relatives, and friends whose lives have been affected by someone else's drinking. Many adults question whether they have been affected by alcoholism. If someone close to you has, or has had a drinking problem, the following questions may help you in determining whether alcoholism affected your childhood or present life and if Al-Anon is for you.

1. Do you constantly seek approval, and affirmation?
2. Do you fail to recognize your accomplishments?
3. Do you fear criticism?
4. Do you overextend yourself?
5. Have you had problems with your own compulsive behavior?
6. Do you have a need for perfection?
7. Are you uneasy when your life is going smoothly, continually anticipating problems?
8. Do you feel more alive in the midst of a crisis?
9. Do you still feel responsible for others, as you did for the problem drinker in your life?
10. Do you care for others easily, yet find it difficult to care for yourself?
11. Do you isolate yourself from other people?
12. Do you respond with fear to authority figures and angry people?

---

*Reprinted with permission of Al-Anon Family Group Headquarters, Inc. from *Did You Grow Up With a Problem Drinker?* ©1984 by Al-Anon Family Group Headquarters, Inc.

13. Do you feel that individuals and society in general are taking advantage of you?

14. Do you have trouble with intimate relationships?

15. Do you confuse pity with love, as you did with the problem drinker?

16. Do you attract and/or seek people who tend to be compulsive and/or abusive?

17. Do you cling to relationships because you are afraid of being alone?

18. Do you often mistrust your own feelings and the feelings expressed by others?

19. Do you find it difficult to identify and express your emotions?

20. Do you think parental drinking may have affected you?

Alcoholism is a family disease. Those of us who have lived with this disease as children sometimes have problems which the Al-Anon program can help us to resolve. If you answered yes to some or all of the above questions, Al-Anon may help. You can contact Al-Anon by checking your local telephone directory or by writing to Al-Anon Family Group Headquarters, Inc.

Artists Recovering through the Twelve Steps Anonymous (A.R.T.S.)
P.O. Box 175
Ansonia Station
New York, NY 10023
A.R.T.S. Hotline at (212) 873-7075
Website: http://www.pagehost.com/ARTS/

Summary*

A.R.T.S. (Artists Recovering through the Twelve Steps) Anonymous is a fellowship of artists who share their experience, strength, and hope with each other that they may recover from their common problem and help others to surrender to their creativity. The only requirement for membership is a desire to fulfill our creative potential. The primary purpose is to express our creative gifts and help others to achieve artistic freedom.

Goal*

To achieve balance between our creative gifts and the demands of everyday living through the practical application of the 12 steps and through the group's support.

Step One*

We admitted we were powerless over our creativity — that our lives had become unmanageable.

---

*Reprinted with permission from A.R.T.S. Anonymous Founder and Public Information Officer. © by A.R.T.S. Anonymous.

Cancer Anonymous (CA)
c/o D. Ecklund
5704 Penny Creek Drive
Austin, TX 78759
Emails only: decklund@ccsi.com or Chris_LS@swbell.net
Website: http://www.ccsi.com/~decklund/CA/

Summary*

An alternate approach — sharing experience, strength, and hope. The Friends Group of Cancer Anonymous was founded in Austin, Texas in 1987 by a small group of people dealing with cancer, either as patients or their loved ones had cancer.

Experience: Our members have either faced cancer in themselves or loved ones.

Strength: We find that coming together on a regular basis with others who are not only surviving, but thriving, helps us to face the rigors and challenges of tests, treatments, and continuing check-ups.

Hope: Sharing through the laughter and the tears helps to change our attitudes.

A 12-step program using the steps, traditions, and concepts of A.A., Alanon, and other sources, Cancer Anonymous seeks to provide a spiritual basis for facing the challenge of cancer.

We are not counselors, medical professionals, nutritionists, etc. We do not, as a group, hold views on any particular treatment or therapy, but do support individual choice. The Friends Group is a gathering of peers.

Chemically Dependent Anonymous (CDA)
CDA Communications, Inc.
General Services Office
P.O. Box 423
Severna Park, MD 21146-0423
C.D.A. Hotline in Annapolis, MD: 1-301-295-3009
C.D.A. Hotline in the Washington, D.C. Metro Area: 1-301-369-6556
Website: http://www.cdaweb.org

Summary*

Chemically Dependent Anonymous deals entirely with the disease of addiction. We of CDA do not make distinctions in the recovery process based on any particular substance, believing that the addictive-compulsive usage of chemicals is the core of our disease and the use of any mood-changing chemical will result in relapse. By sharing our experience, strength, and hope with each other, we solve our common problem and help others to recover from chemical dependence which has made their lives unmanageable.

Goal

To abstain from all mind-altering chemicals.

Self-Assessment Questions*

1. Has chemical use caused you financial difficulties?

2. Have you lost time from work due to the use of chemicals?

3. Do you use chemicals to build up your self-confidence?

4. Have you ever had a complete loss of memory while under the influence of chemicals?

5. Do you crave chemicals?

6. Has chemical use caused unhappiness in your home life?

7. Have you ever been treated by a physician for chemical use?

8. Do you ever feel remorseful after using?

9. Do chemicals make you careless of your family's welfare?

10. Has chemical use affected your reputation?

11. Do you associate with lower companions and an inferior environment when you are using?

---

12. Do you get high to escape from your worries or troubles?

13. Has using put your job, schooling, or business in jeopardy?

14. Do you use chemicals daily?

15. Do you need to get loaded to have a good time?

16. Do you use chemicals when you are alone?

17. Have you ever been in an institution or a hospital due to the use of chemicals?

18. Are you ashamed of your behavior after using?

19. Does chemical use decrease your ambition?

20. Do you feel bad when you are not using a chemical?

If you answered yes to three or more of these questions, this indicates that you have a problem with chemicals. Only you can make that statement about yourself."

Cleptomaniacs and Shoplifters Anonymous (CASA)
CASA
810 Spring Street
Ann Arbor, MI 48103
For more info call Terry at (734) 913-6990
Email: shulmann@umich.edu
Website: http://www-personal.umich.edu/~shulmann/CASA/

Summary*

Cleptomaniacs and Shoplifters Anonymous (CASA) is a unique, independent, and secular weekly self-help group founded in Detroit, Mich. in September 1992 by a recovering shoplifter who felt such a group could help himself, others, and the community as a whole. CASA's purpose is to provide a safe, confidential, and non-judgmental space for compassion, understanding, and recovery from "addictive-compulsive" dishonest behavior, primarily shoplifting, fraud, cleptomania, and embezzlement. CASA's goal is to educate individuals in the group and the community at large about the complex motivations and recovery treatment process for these behaviors, while emphasizing personal responsibility and accountability.

CASA is a non-profit, self-run, self-help group made up of a diverse group of persons with a mix of voluntary and court-ordered attendees.

Common reasons why people shoplift/steal:

- to express feelings of anger, revenge, or entitlement,
- to fill a sense of emptiness due to grief or loss,
- to try to make life seem fair,
- as a thrill or high to escape problems, numb feelings, or ease depression.

What are CASA meetings like?

While every meeting is unique, the basic structure allows each person to express his or her feelings, circumstances, and own insights about the behavior and how to stop it. We learn from hearing ourselves, as well as listening to others. Laughter and tears, questions and comments, and engaging dialogue are all common.

Who attends CASA?

- Men and women from teen to senior
- Career professionals, lay persons, and homemakers
- Recent and habitual shoplifters/cleptomaniacs
- Family and friends of group members

---

*Reprinted with permission from Cleptomaniacs and Shoplifters Anonymous. © 1992 by Cleptomaniacs and Shoplifters Anonymous.

- Occasional guests such as therapists, attorneys, or students
- Anyone who wants to understand these behaviors and control them

We can help people help themselves:

- overcome legal troubles
- strengthen sense of self
- heal emotional wounds
- rebuild relationships
- live more honestly and peacefully
- increase self-control and self-awareness
- experience great joy
- feel
- help others

Clutterers Anonymous (CLA)
World Service Organization
P.O. Box 25884
Santa Ana, CA 92799-5884

Summary*

A fellowship of individuals who help each other solve their common problem with clutter. They share their experience, strength, and hope with others to help them recover. If there's no local meeting and you cannot start one, you can receive the latest issue of the quarterly newsletter by sending a business-sized self-addressed stamped envelope.

Primary Purpose*

Our primary purpose is to eliminate clutter, to establish more order in our lives, and to carry this message of recovery to clutterers who still suffer (CLA Preamble).

Self-Assessment Questions —
How Do I Know If I'm a Clutterer?*

1. Do you have more possessions or items in your life than you can handle comfortably?

2. Do you find it difficult to dispose of many things, even those you haven't used in years?

3. Do you rent storage space to house items you never use?

4. Do you spend time looking for things that are hard to find because of all the clutter?

5. Do you find it easier to drop something than to put it away, or to wedge an object into an overcrowded drawer or closet rather than to find a space for it?

6. Do you collect things to give to others?

7. Do you bring things into your house without establishing a place for them?

8. Is your clutter causing problems in your relationships?

9. Are you embarrassed to have visitors because your home is never presentable?

10. Do you hesitate sharing about this problem because you are ashamed of your cluttering?

11. Are you constantly doing for others while your own home is out of order?

12. Do you miss deadlines or abandon projects because you can't find the paperwork or material you need to finish the work?

13. Do you sometimes get buried in details, making projects take much longer than is really necessary?

14. Do you procrastinate about cleaning up because you believe you must do it perfectly or you won't do it at all?

15. Are you easily side-tracked, moving from one project to another without finishing any of them?

16. Do you have problems with time management and estimating how long it takes to do things?

17. Do you believe there is all the time in the world to clean your house, finish those projects, and read all those piles of old magazines?

18. Do you use distractions to escape from your clutter?

19. Have you tried to clean up from time to time but find yourself unable to stick with it?

20. Does the problem appear to be growing?

If you answered yes to three or more of these questions, there is a chance you are a clutterer or well on your way to becoming one.

Cocaine Anonymous (CA)
World Services, Inc.
P.O. Box 2000
Los Angeles, CA 90049-8000
Telephone: (310) 559-5833
Fax: (310) 559-2554
Email: cawso@ca.org
Public Information Email: pubinfo@ca.org
Website: http://www.ca.org/

Summary

A program for people of all ages who are addicted or suspect they may be addicted to cocaine and/or all other mind-altering substances.

Goal

Total abstinence from cocaine and all other mind-altering substances.

Self-Assessment Questions*

1. Do you ever use more cocaine than you planned?

2. Has the use of cocaine interfered with your job?

3. Is your cocaine use causing conflict with your spouse or family?

4. Do you feel depressed, guilty, or remorseful after you use cocaine?

5. Do you use whatever cocaine you have almost continuously until the supply is exhausted?

6. Have you ever experienced sinus problems or nosebleeds due to cocaine use?

7. Do you ever wish that you had never taken that first line, hit, or injection of cocaine?

8. Have you experienced chest pains or rapid or irregular heartbeats when using cocaine?

9. Do you have an obsession to get cocaine when you don't have it?

10. Are you experiencing financial difficulties due to your cocaine use?

11. Do you experience an anticipation-high just knowing you are about to use cocaine?

12. After using cocaine, do you have difficulty sleeping without taking a drink or another drug?

---

*Reprinted with permission from Cocaine Anonymous World Services, Inc. ©1992 by Cocaine Anonymous World Services, Inc.

13. Are you absorbed with the thought of getting loaded even while interacting with a friend or loved one?

14. Have you begun to use drugs or drink alone?

15. Do you ever have feelings that people are talking about you or watching you?

16. Do you use larger doses of drugs or alcohol to get the same high you once experienced?

17. Have you tried to quit or cut down on your cocaine use only to find that you couldn't?

18. Have any of your friends or family suggested that you may have a problem?

19. Have you ever lied to or misled those around you about how much or how often you use?

20. Do you use drugs in your car, at work, in the bathroom, on airplanes, or other public places?

21. Are you afraid that if you stop using cocaine or alcohol your work will suffer or you will lose your energy, motivation, or confidence?

22. Do you spend time with people or in places you otherwise would not be around but for the availability of drugs?

23. Have you ever stolen drugs or money from friends or family?

If you have answered yes to any of these questions, you may have a cocaine problem. There is an answer . . . come to meetings of Cocaine Anonymous, read the literature and join us . . . we want to help.

Co-Anon Family Groups, Inc. (Co-Anon)
P.O. Box 64742-66
Los Angeles, CA 90064
Telephone: (310) 859-2206
Leave Messages: (818) 377-4317

Summary*

Co-Anon Family Groups are a fellowship of men and women who are husbands, wives, parents, relatives, or close friends of someone who is chemically dependent. If someone is seeking a solution to the problems that come from living with a practicing or recovering cocaine addict, Co-Anon can help them.

Goal

To surrender trying to control the addict and deal with the impact the cocaine addiction has made on their own lives, as well as deal with the issues of their lives.

Self-Assessment Questions**

Millions of people are affected by the cocaine addiction of someone else. The following questions are designed to help you decide whether or not Co-Anon is for you.

1. Do you try to monitor someone else's cocaine use?

2. Is your main concern how to get someone else to stop using cocaine?

3. Do you have money problems because of someone else's cocaine use?

4. Do you feel your problem is unlike anyone else's?

5. Do you threaten to leave the addict if they don't stop using?

6. Do you feel if the addict stopped using, the problem would go away?

7. Do you search for hidden vials, razor blades, straws, paraphernalia?

8. Do you feel like your life is in order and only the addict has a problem?

9. Have you considered calling the addict's dealers, the authorities, an intervention unit?

10. Do you feel that if the addict really loved you they would stop using cocaine because you asked them to?

11. Do you tell lies to cover up the addict's using?

---

12. Are you afraid to speak up on certain issues for fear the addict will use more, blame you, or hurt you?

13. Have you lost material possessions to support the addict's using?

14. Do you resent coming to a Co-Anon meeting because the addict will not attend Cocaine Anonymous meetings?

15. Do you feel confused about how to handle the situations relating to cocaine or the addict's behavior?

16. Do you want to force the addict to attend Cocaine Anonymous meetings?

17. Do you want to know how to deal with your son's/daughter's problem with cocaine?

18. Do you hope that each time you see or hear of the addict's use will be the last time?

19. Does the addict make seemingly honest promises that never materialize?

20. Do you wait up at night or lose sleep waiting for the addict to come home?

If you answered yes to four or more questions, then Co-Anon is for you. Attend as many meetings as possible and use the Co-Anon lifeline to find out more — you are in the right place.

CoDependents Anonymous (CoDA)
Fellowship Services Office
P.O. Box 33577
Phoenix, AZ 85067-3577
Telephone: 602/277-7991
Website: www.ourcoda.org

Summary — Welcome to CoDependents Anonymous®

We welcome you to CoDependents Anonymous, a program of recovery from codependence, where each of us may share our experience, strength, and hope in our efforts to find freedom where there has been bondage and peace where there has been turmoil in our relationships with others and ourselves.

Most of us have been searching for ways to overcome the dilemmas of the conflicts in our relationships and our childhoods. Many of us were raised in families where addictions existed — some of us were not. In either case, we have found in each of our lives that codependence is a most deeply-rooted compulsive behavior and that it is born out of our sometimes moderately-, sometimes extremely-dysfunctional family systems. We have each experienced in our own ways the painful trauma of the emptiness of our childhood and relationships throughout our lives.

We attempted to use others — our mates, friends, and even our children, as our sole source of identity, value, and well-being, and as a way of trying to restore within us the emotional losses from our childhoods. Our histories may include other powerful addictions which, at times we have used to cope with our codependence.

We have all learned to survive life, but in CoDA we are learning to live life. Through applying the 12-steps and principles found in CoDA to our daily life and relationships — both present and past — we can experience a new freedom from our self-defeating lifestyles. It is an individual growth process. Each of us is growing at our own pace and will continue to do so as we remain open to God's will for us on a daily basis. Our sharing is our way of identification and helps us to free the emotional bonds of our past and the compulsive control of our present.

No matter how traumatic your past or despairing your present may seem, there is hope for a new day in the program of CoDependents Anonymous. No longer do you need to rely on others as a power greater than yourself. May you instead find here a new strength within to be that which God intended — precious and free.

---

*Reprinted with permission of the CoDependents Anonymous Board of Directors from CoDependents Anonymous' website.

Patterns of Codependency*

Denial Patterns:

- I have difficulty identifying what I am feeling.
- I minimize, alter, or deny how I truly feel.
- I perceive myself as completely unselfish and dedicated to the well-being of others.

Low Self-Esteem Patterns:

- I have difficulty making decisions.
- I judge everything I think, say or do harshly, as never "good enough."
- I am embarrassed to receive recognition and praise or gifts.
- I do not ask others to meet my needs or desires.
- I value others' approval of my thinking, feelings, and behavior over my own.
- I do not perceive myself as a lovable or worthwhile person.

Compliance Patterns:

- I compromise my own values and integrity to avoid rejection or others' anger.
- I am very sensitive to how others are feeling and feel the same.
- I am extremely loyal, remaining in harmful situations too long.
- I value others' opinions and feelings more than my own and am afraid to express differing opinions and feelings of my own.
- I put aside my own interests and hobbies in order to do what others want. I accept sex when I want love.

Control Patterns:

- I believe most other people are incapable of taking care of themselves.
- I attempt to convince others of what they "should" think and how they "truly" feel.
- I become resentful when others will not let me help them.
- I freely offer others advice and directions without being asked.
- I lavish gifts and favors on those I care about.
- I use sex to gain approval and acceptance.
- I have to be "needed" in order to have a relationship with others.

---

*Reprinted with permission of the CoDependents Anonymous Board of Directors from CoDependents Anonymous' website.

Codependents of Sexual Addiction Anonymous (COSA)
COSA National Service Organization
9337-B Katy Hwy. #142
Houston, TX 77024 USA
(612) 537-6904
Website: http://www2.shore.net/~cosa/

Summary*
Codependents of Sexual Addiction is open to anyone whose life has been affected by another person's compulsive sexual behavior. It is a 12-step recovery program for men and women who are sexually codependent. In COSA, we find hope whether or not there is a sexually-addicted person currently in our lives. COSA recognizes that sexual co-addiction is a disease with effects as devastating as sexual addiction. With the humble act of reaching out, we begin the process of recovery.

Self-Assessment Questions — Key Identifying Behaviors*
The following questions can be used to help you identify sexually codependent behaviors and assess your need for the COSA program. Do you:

1. Find yourself trying to control a partner, relative, friend, employer, or colleague's sexual actions or thoughts?

2. Allow sex to play a dominant or all-consuming role in your relationships?

3. Think things would be better if only you performed better sexually?

4. Find sex more uncomfortable than pleasurable?

5. Withdraw emotionally, have your mind on other things during sex, or feel empty afterwards?

6. Focus more on another person's sexual attitudes, beliefs, or needs than your own?

7. Use sex to try to repair relationships when they are strained?

8. Find yourself engaging in compulsive or depressive behaviors to avoid your feelings (sleeping too much, losing sleep, eating poorly, overeating, overspending, or abusing chemicals)?

9. Participate in unhealthy or degrading relationships for fear of being alone?

10. Compare your appearance with others (co-workers, friends, celebrities)?

---

*Reprinted with permission of the National Service Organization of COSA. © National Service Organization of COSA. Permission to reprint this material does not mean that COSA has reviewed or approved this document.

11. Avoid speaking with others (friends, a professional counselor) about your sexual behaviors or feelings?

12. Engage in sexual activities with your partner that feel disturbing or shaming?

13. Get accused of or feel that you are "frigid" or "not with it" sexually?

14. Lie about your sexual feelings or reactions in order to please your partner (fake orgasm)?

15. Neglect your needs, or those of family and friends, to comply with your partner's sexual desires?

16. Play detective (look through belongings, check whereabouts, etc.) to find clues of a partner, relative, or friend's sexual acting out?

Compulsive Eaters Anonymous-How (CEA-HOW)
San Diego County Intergroup
P.O. Box 900894
San Diego, Ca. 92190
(619) 543-8961
Website: http://www.ceahow.com

Summary

CEA-HOW is a fellowship of men and women who meet to share their experience, strength, and hope with one another in order that they may solve their common problem and help those who still suffer to recover from compulsive eating. HOW meetings offer a disciplined and structured approach to the compulsive eater who accepts the 12 steps and 12 traditions as a program of recovery. Our primary purpose is to stop eating compulsively . . . and we welcome in fellowship and friendly understanding all those who share our common problem.

Self-Assessment Questions — Are You a Compulsive Eater?*

1. Do you eat when you're not hungry?

2. Do you go on eating binges for no apparent reason?

3. Do you have feelings of guilt and remorse after overeating?

4. Do you give too much time and thought to food?

5. Do you look forward with pleasure and anticipation to the moments when you can eat alone?

6. Do you plan these secret binges ahead of time?

7. Do you eat sensibly before others and make up for it alone?

8. Is your weight affecting the way you live your life?

9. Have you tried to diet for a week (or longer), only to fall short of your goal?

10. Do you resent others telling you to "use a little willpower" to stop overeating?

11. Despite evidence to the contrary, have you continued to assert that you can diet "on your own" whenever you wish?

12. Do you crave food at a definite time, day or night, other than mealtimes?

13. Do you eat to escape from worries or trouble?

14. Have you ever been treated for obesity or a food-related condition?

15. Does your eating behavior make you or others unhappy?

---

*Reprinted with permission from Compulsive Eaters Anonymous-How (CEA-HOW). © 1997 by Compulsive Eaters Anonymous-How.

Have you answered yes to three or more of these questions? If so, it is probable that you have or are well on the way to having a compulsive eating problem. We have found that the way to arrest this progressive disease is to practice the 12-step recovery program of Compulsive Eaters Anonymous-HOW.

Crystal Meth Anonymous (CMA)
Los Angeles 213-488-4455
San Francisco 415-267-5933
Website: http://members.xoom.com/CMA/

Summary — CMA . . . A Members View*

Where is there hope? Where can I go to find men and women who care if I live or die? Where is the exit from this cold, cold place to which my use of speed has brought me? If you are asking yourself these questions, the fellowship of Crystal Meth Anonymous (CMA) offers one of several solutions to your problem.

Over the years, several people in recovery noticed the necessity for a 12-step program tailored to the needs of people addicted to crystal meth (speed, crank) if only to serve as an entry into the recovery community. We noticed that there were many people uncomfortable and fidgety in 12-step meetings. They were often very disruptive. They were different. Our experience taught us that without being able to identify with addicts at meetings or in the fellowship, recovery was very difficult. We cannot share our experiences in a vacuum. CMA came into being to address this issue. We gather together that we may know that we are not alone and that there are many more people like us who have survived. This is the central issue of the CMA program. At CMA we provide a safe environment for recovering addicts to come and address their fears, share their hopes, and seek a solution to their problem. Along with sharing our experience, strength, and hope, our daily lives provide evidence to the addict seeking recovery, that there is a way out of addiction to crystal meth.

There is no mystery to it. CMA uses the 12 steps of Alcoholics Anonymous along with fellowship and CMA meetings to provide a structure of recovery. Over time our experience has shown that one addict working with another can begin the process by which we can stay clean one day at a time.

Debtors Anonymous (DA)
General Service Office
P.O. Box 888
Needham, MA 02492-0009
(781) 453-2743
Email: (Media and professionals) pi@debtoranonymous.org
Email: (Newcomers) new@debtorsanonymous.org
Email: (Current DA members) mem@debtorsanonymous.org
International Contact: London, UK (telephone) 014269 47150
Website: http://www.debtorsanonymous.org/

Summary

A fellowship where the common problem is compulsively getting into debt. The only requirement for membership is a desire to stop incurring unsecured debt.

Goal

To abstain from borrowing or charging and to recover from this addiction.

Self-Assessment Questions*

Most compulsive debtors will answer yes to at least eight out of the following 15 questions.

1. Are your debts making your home life unhappy?
2. Does the pressure of your debts distract you from your daily work?
3. Are your debts affecting your reputation?
4. Do your debts cause you to think less of yourself?
5. Have you ever given false information in order to obtain credit?
6. Have you ever made unrealistic promises to your creditors?
7. Does the pressure of your debts make you careless of the welfare of your family?
8. Do you ever fear that your employer, family, or friends will learn the extent of your total indebtedness?
9. When faced with a difficult financial situation, does the prospect of borrowing give you an inordinate feeling of relief?
10. Does the pressure of your debts cause you to have difficulty in sleeping?
11. Has the pressure of your debts ever caused you to consider getting drunk?

---

*Reprinted with permission from *Debtors Anonymous*, Debtors Anonymous General Service Office. © 1982 by Debtors Anonymous General Service Office.

12. Have you ever borrowed money without giving adequate consideration to the rate of interest you are required to pay?

13. Do you usually expect a negative response when you are subject to a credit investigation?

14. Have you ever developed a strict regimen for paying off your debts, only to break it under pressure?

15. Do you justify your debts by telling yourself that you are superior to the "other" people, and when you get your "break," you'll be out of debt overnight?

How did you score? If you answered yes to eight or more of these questions, the chances are that you have a problem with compulsive debt, or are well on your way to having one. If this is the case, today can be a turning point in your life.

We have all arrived at this crossroads. One road, a soft road, lures you on to further despair, illness, ruin, and in some cases, mental institutions, prison, or suicide. The other road, a more challenging road, leads to self-respect, solvency, healing, and personal fulfillment. We urge you to take the first difficult step onto the more solid road now.

Business Owners Debtors Anonymous (BODA)
c/o Debtors Anonymous
General Service Office
P.O. Box 888
Needham, MA 02492-0009
(781) 453-2743
Email: (Media and professionals) pi@debtoranonymous.org
Email: (Newcomers)new@debtorsanonymous.org
Email: (Current DA members) mem@debtorsanonymous.org
International Contact: London, UK (telephone) 014269 47150
Website: http://www.boda.org
Alternative Website: http://www.debtorsanonymous.org/

Summary*

By vote of the 1997 Debtors Anonymous World Conference, Business Owners Debtors Anonymous became an integral part of Debtors Anonymous. BODA groups are encouraged to register with the Debtors Anonymous General Service Board and Debtors Anonymous groups, and to send voting representatives to the annual Debtors Anonymous World Conference.

*Reprinted with permission from Debt-Anon Family Groups Board of Trustees from Business Owners Debtors Anonymous website.

Debt-Anon Family Groups, Inc.
c/o Debtors Anonymous
General Service Office
P.O. Box 888
Needham, MA 02492-0009
(781) 453-2743
Email: (Media and professionals) pi@debtoranonymous.org
Email: (Newcomers) new@debtorsanonymous.org
Email: (Current DA members) mem@debtorsanonymous.org
International Contact: London, UK (telephone) 014269 47150
Website: http://www.debtorsanonymous.org/

Summary

A 12-step fellowship for co-debtors. The only requirement for membership is that there is a problem of compulsive debting with someone important to that member.

Goal

To help families and friends of compulsive debtors. This is done by practicing the 12 steps themselves and by welcoming and giving comfort to families of compulsive debtors.

Self-Assessment Questions*

1. Do you worry about how much money someone else owes?

2. Do you have money problems because of someone else's debting?

3. Do you tell lies to cover up for someone else's debting?

4. Do you feel that if the debtor loved you, she or he would stop debting?

5. Are family plans or routines often upset by the debtor's behavior?

6. Do you avoid money discussions with the debtor because of fear that he or she will get angry or will go on a spending spree?

7. Have you privately hurt or publicly embarrassed by the debtor's words or actions?

8. Do you sometimes feel like a failure when you think of the lengths you have gone to control the debtor's financial behavior?

---

*Reprinted with permission from Debt-Anon Family Groups. © by Debt-Anon Family Groups.

9. Do you think that if the debtor became solvent, your other problems would be solved?

10. Do you often feel angry, confused, or depressed?

11. Do you feel that there is no one who understands your problems?

Depressed Anonymous (DA)
Dr. Hugh Smith, Coordinator
P.O. Box 17414
Louisville, KY 40217
(502) 569-1989
(Please include a self-addressed, stamped envelope)
Email: info@depressedanon.com
Website: http://www.depressedanon.com

Summary*

Depressed Anonymous has been formed with the idea that mutual aid empowers people and is a therapeutic healing force. This organization helps to form groups or circles of support for persons depressed.

They offer depressed individual information on how to gain and use the tools for overcoming depression. Groups have been formed throughout the United States and several have been successfully organized in other international communities as well.

These groups are similar, in methodology and goal, to those used by Alcoholics Anonymous in its work in helping alcoholic individuals. The members learn that they have a choice to stay depressed or to take responsibility for themselves and leave the prison of depression.

As a part of forming these groups, Depressed Anonymous seeks to inform and educate the public about the signs and symptoms of depression, inform them of where they can go to seek help and to help establish self-help programs in their communities. We also visit the various health-care administrators and caregivers to inform them of the resources that we can offer and to aid us by locating the depressed patient and thereby give them hope.

Depressed Anonymous aims to be a link between the mental health care communities and those suffering from depression. Depressed Anonymous will provide its many educational and advocacy resources to professionals so that they may provide their patients with hope and real help.

Self-Assessment Inventory

Use this inventory to see if you might be depressed, check those that you have experienced over the past two weeks.

☐ Have you had a change in appetite (15 lb. weight gain or 15 lb. weight loss)?

☐ Shifts in sleeping patterns (too much sleep or not enough)? Waking up early?

---

*Reprinted with permission from Dr. Hugh Smith, Coordinator, Depressed Anonymous. ©1997 by Depressed Anonymous.

☐ Tired all the time?

☐ Agitated or increased activity? Always on the go?

☐ Loss of interest in daily activities and/or decreased sexual drive?

☐ Withdrawing from others and wanting to be alone most of the time?

☐ Weeping/not being able to cry?

☐ Lapses of memory?

☐ Indecisiveness?

☐ Fear of losing one's mind?

☐ Reluctance to take risks?

☐ Suicidal thoughts?

If you or someone you know is experiencing at least four of these signs of depression for more than two weeks Depressed Anonymous might be helpful.

Drugs Anonymous (Renamed: Pills Anonymous)
Pills Anonymous
P.O. Box 1031
New York, NY 10028-0003
(212) 874-0700

Summary

Twelve-step program renamed Pills Anonymous. See Pills Anonymous (PA) for details.

Dual Recovery Anonymous (DRA)
Dual Recovery Anonymous Central Service Office
1302 Division Street, Suite 100
Nashville, Tenn. 37203
(615) 742-1000
Toll Free: 888/869-9230
Fax: (615) 297-9346
Website: http://www.dualdiagnosis.org

Dual Recovery Anonymous Newsletter
P.O. Box 67424
Scotts Valley, CA 95067
Fax: (615) 483-5564

Summary*

DRA is an independent, self-help organization. Their goal is to help men and women who experience a dual illness. We are chemically dependent and we are also affected by an emotional or mental illness. Both illnesses affect us in all areas of our lives: physically, mentally, socially, and spiritually.

The primary purpose of DRA is to help one another achieve dual recovery, to prevent relapse, and to carry the message of recovery to others who experience dual disorders.

DRA has two requirements for membership: a desire to stop using alcohol and other intoxicating drugs and a desire to manage our emotional or psychiatric illness in a healthy and constructive way.

DRA is a nonprofessional self-help program. There must always be a clear boundary separating the work of DRA from the work of chemical dependency and mental-health professionals. The DRA fellowship has no opinion on matters of diagnosis, treatment, medication, or other issues related to the health-care professions. The DRA fellowship is not affiliated with any other self-help organization or 12-step program. DRA has no opinion on the way other groups address the problems of dual disorders and dual recovery. We do not criticize the efforts of others. The DRA central service office will offer support to others who wish to start DRA meetings and who wish to work with other groups to carry the message.

Accepting Differences

Newcomers and visitors may ask, can a DRA program help me even with the type of symptoms that I have? Such feelings are not uncommon. We need to help newcomers recognize that a variety of symptoms are possible with a dual illness. There is no single type of dual disorder.

Some of us feared that we were becoming hopelessly impaired. We came to believe that we would never be "normal" again. Many of us experienced great shame and guilt. We believed that our emotional or psychiatric illness and chemical dependency were our fault.

Some of us have become secretive. We tried to keep our drinking and drug use a secret, and later some of us felt a need to keep our recovery and steps a secret. We also felt our psychiatric illness **must** be kept secret, especially if our recovery program included prescription medication.

We seemed to run out of ways to protect our feelings and self-esteem, and to protect ourselves from the attitudes of those around us. Many of us gradually went into a closet of denial. If there are any among us who have felt as though they were living in that closet, we welcome you. We want you to know that the fear, isolation, and secrecy no longer need to be a part of your life.

The 12 Steps of DRA*

1. Admitted we were powerless over our dual illness of chemical dependency and emotional or psychiatric illness — that our lives had become unmanageable.

2. Came to believe that a Higher Power of our understanding could restore us to sanity.

3. Made a decision to turn our will and our lives over to the care of our Higher Power, to help us rebuild our lives in a positive and caring way.

4. Made a searching and fearless inventory of ourselves.

5. Admitted to our Higher Power, to ourselves, and to another human being, the exact nature of our assets and our liabilities.

6. Were entirely ready to have our Higher Power remove our liabilities.

7. Humbly asked our Higher Power to remove these liabilities and to help us strengthen our assets for recovery.

8. Made a list of all persons we had harmed and became willing to make amends to them all.

---

9. Made direct amends to such people whenever possible, except when to do so would injure them or others.

10. Continued to take personal inventory and when wrong promptly admitted it, while continuing to recognize our progress in dual recovery.

11. Sought through prayer and meditation to improve our conscious contact with our Higher Power, praying only for knowledge of our Higher Power's will for us and the power to carry that out.

12. Having had a spiritual awakening as a result of these steps, we try to carry this message to others who experience dual disorders and to practice these principles in all our affairs.

DRA Suggested Reading List

- Hamilton, Timothy. "Dual Recovery Anonymous: A Blueprint," *Dual Disorders Recovery Book.* Center City, Minn.: Hazelden, 1994.

- Samples, Pat, and Timothy Hamilton. "Duel Recovery Anonymous: Meeting Format," *12 Steps and Dual Disorders.* Center City, Minn.: Hazelden, 1994.

Emotions Anonymous (EA)
Emotions Anonymous International
P.O. Box 4245
St. Paul, MN 55104-0245
Telephone: (651) 647-9712
Fax (651) 647-1593
Email: eaisc@mtn.org
Website: http://www.emotionsanonymous.org

Summary*

This fellowship is composed of people who come together in weekly meetings with the purpose of working toward recovery from emotional difficulties. EA members are from many walks of life and are of diverse ages, economic status, social and educational backgrounds. The only requirement for membership is a desire to become well emotionally.

Emotions Anonymous has been known to work miracles in the lives of many who suffer from problems as diverse as: depression, anger, broken or strained relationships, grief, anxiety, low self-esteem, panic, abnormal fears, resentment, jealousy, guilt, despair, fatigue, tension, boredom, loneliness, withdrawal, obsessive and negative thinking, worry, compulsive behavior, and a variety of other emotional issues.

Goal

To achieve and maintain emotional well-being, as well as develop coping skills using the 12 steps.

Families Anonymous, Inc. (FA)
World Service Office
P.O. Box 528
Van Nuys, CA 91408
(818) 989-7841
1-800-736-9805

Summary

A fellowship of relatives and friends of people involved in the abuse of mind-altering substances or exhibiting related behavioral problems such as runaways, delinquents, underachievers, etc.

Goal

Develop new ways to deal with the everyday stresses of coping with a substance abuser or a loved one deep in the habit of unacceptable behavior.

Self-Assessment Questions*

1. Do you lie awake worrying about your child? (whatever age)?
2. Do you feel frustrated in your attempts to control your child?
3. Do you disapprove of your youngster's lifestyle?
4. Do you argue with your child about his or her friends?
5. Do you find it increasingly difficult to communicate with your child?
6. Does your child's behavior have you "climbing the walls"?
7. Do you often ask, "Where have I failed"?
8. Do you feel it necessary to protect your child because he's unusually sensitive, etc.?
9. Are you trying to compensate for some family misfortune — divorce, death, illness, etc.?
10. Are you embarrassed to discuss your situation with your friends or relatives?
11. Do you find yourself lying or covering up for your child?
12. Do you feel resentful or hostile toward your child?
13. Do you find it increasingly difficult to trust your child?
14. Do you worry about your child's behavior affecting other members of the family?

---

*Reprinted with permission from Families Anonymous, Inc. © by Families Anonymous, Inc.

15. Do you blame your spouse for your child's problems?

16. Do you blame yourself?

17. Are your child's problems starting to undermine your marriage?

18. Do you find yourself playing detective, fearful of what you'll find?

19. Do you go from place to place seeking help for your child?

20. Is concern for your child giving you headaches, stomachaches, or heartache?

If you answered yes to any three of these questions, this is an early-warning sign. If you answered yes to any four, chances are that you could use some help. If you answered yes to five or more, you are definitely in need of help.

Fear of Success Anonymous (FOSA)
16161 Ventura Blvd., #727
Encino, California 91436
(818) 907-3953
http://ourworld.compuserve.com/homepages/fosa/

Summary*

We commit to a positive program of daily actions toward goals of our choosing. We celebrate our individual commitment, one day at a time, towards the realization of our goals by receiving chips and candles for continuous back-to-back days of action. We celebrate 30 days, 60 days, 90 days, six months, nine months, and yearly birthdays of positive action to recover from the fear of success.

The only requirement for F.O.S.A. membership is a desire to succeed, as we individually define success.

Self-Assessment Questions

1. Do you feel frustrated and "stuck" with your present life?

2. Are you waiting for someone to rescue you from your problems and/or for a "perfect" time to do something?

3. Do you spend lots of time daydreaming about a better life?

4. Do you believe that success is mostly luck and for other people, but not you?

5. Are you able to accept the good that comes your way without feeling it is "undeserved?"

6. Do you treat your mistakes as feedback without condemning yourself?

7. When you succeed, do you discount your efforts?

8. Are you afraid to take risks in your career or your personal life?

9. Do you feel compelled to seek the approval of others?

10. Do you self-sabotage by: over-scheduling, rushing, procrastinating, consistent tardiness, workaholism, dressing inappropriately, inadequate preparation, poor planning, tactless behavior?

11. Is it hard for you to enjoy good fortune because you're afraid that disaster is inevitable?

12. Do you feel that you will never get it all together or that your best years are behind you?

---

*Reprinted with permission from Fear of Success Anonymous, Inc. © by Fear of Success Anonymous, Inc.

13. Do you fail to live in the present, but instead dwell mostly in the past or the future?

14. Do you constantly complain, rather than take action to resolve your problems?

15. Do you feel that even if you really tried your best, you would fail?

16. Are you constantly unable to make up your mind as to what you really want?

17. Are you attracted to people who don't appreciate and accept you as you are?

18. Do you discount your accomplishments rather than celebrate them?

19. Are you uncomfortable when given a compliment or present?

20. Once you have achieved a level of success, do you consistently destroy it through self-sabotage?

21. Do you tell yourself that your dreams are "unrealistic" and refuse to write them down or take action on them?

If you answered yes to three or more of these questions, you probably suffer from the fear of success.

The cofounders, Les and Gerry, each had recovery in other 12-step programs but felt elements of their lives and careers were still out of control because of self-sabotage. Since the 12 steps had worked in other areas of their lives, they decided to see if they could be applied to their fear of success. They set about creating a 12-step program based upon faith and predicated on action. They committed to writing out their long-term and immediate goals and committing them to their Higher Power and to another person. They agreed to write out a daily plan of action and commit to it, using the tools of the program to remain in action when the fear threatened to overwhelm them. Our co-founders attained success in their own lives and founded F.O.S.A. in order to maintain their recovery and carry the message to others who suffer from the fear of success.

Fellowship of Depressives Anonymous (FDA)
329 East 62nd Street
New York, NY 10021
(212) 689-2600 (answering service only)

Central Address: 36 Chestnut Avenue,
Beverley, East Yorkshire, UK
HU17 9QU
Email: dle@wavenet.co.uk
http://www.ribblewebdesign.co.uk/fda/

Summary*

A fellowship of people who help each other to overcome their common problems of anxiousness and depression. The fellowship of Depressives Anonymous is a charity that aims to ease the burden of depression, by sharing it. It is run entirely by its members, who are all either sufferers or ex-sufferers of depression. Members can share their experiences in different ways. They can write to the quarterly newsletter, remaining anonymous if they wish, this is a good way of circulating ideas among our membership. They also operate a pen-friend scheme, to put people with similar interests and viewpoints in touch. Having regular contact with someone who understands exactly how you feel can be a real boost. The FDA has quite a few groups around the country, all run by members. They feel that receiving sympathy and support from others, as well as giving it, can be enormously helpful, especially during the bad times.

Goal

To change troublesome behavior patterns and attitudes about living.

Food Addicts Anonymous (FAA)
FAA World Service Office
4623 Forest Hill Blvd, Suite 109-4
West Palm Beach, FL 33415-9120
Telephone: (561) 967-3871
Email: normajean-Phillip@keybank.com
Website: http://www.erols.com/randrc/faa/

Summary*

Food Addicts Anonymous is a fellowship of men and women who are willing to recover from the disease of food addiction. Sharing our experience, strength, and hope with others allows us to recover from this disease, one day at a time.

Food Addicts Anonymous is self-supporting through our own contributions. We are not affiliated with any diet or weight-loss programs, treatment facilities, or religious organizations. We neither endorse nor oppose any causes. Our primary purpose is to stay abstinent and to help other food addicts achieve abstinence.

Food Addicts Anonymous was founded in December 1987, in West Palm Beach, Florida. Our founder is a wonderful woman named Judith C. We are very grateful to Judith C. for starting our "familyship."

The FAA program is based on the belief that food addiction is a biochemical disease. By following a food plan devoid of all addictive substances, we can recover. These substances include sugar, flour, and wheat in all their forms. They also include fats and any other high-carbohydrate, refined, processed foods that cause us problems individually.

Our primary purpose is to stay abstinent and to help other food addicts achieve abstinence. We invite you to join us on the road to recovery and suggest you attend six meetings before you decide you don't need our help. You need to know that withdrawal is a necessary part of recovery.

We can get better if we continue to follow our food plan, work the tools of the program, and ask for help.

Gamblers Anonymous (GA)
International Service Office
P.O. Box 17173
Los Angeles, CA 90017
Telephone: (213) 386-8789
Fax: (213) 386-0030
Website: http://www.gamblersanonymous.org
Email: isomain@gamblersanonymous.org

Summary

An international fellowship of compulsive gamblers who have not been able to stop the destructive gambling pattern alone.

Goal

To stop compulsive gambling.

Self-Assessment Questions*

1. Did you ever lose time from work or school due to gambling?

2. Has gambling ever made your home life unhappy?

3. Did gambling affect your reputation?

4. Have you ever felt remorse after gambling?

5. Did you ever gamble to get money with which to pay debts or otherwise solve financial difficulties?

6. Did gambling cause a decrease in your ambition or efficiency?

7. After losing, did you feel you must return as soon as possible and win back your losses?

8. After a win, did you have a strong urge to return and win more?

9. Did you often gamble until your last dollar was gone?

10. Did you ever borrow to finance your gambling?

11. Have you ever sold anything to finance gambling?

12. Were you reluctant to use "gambling money" for normal expenditures?

13. Did gambling make you careless of the welfare of your family?

14. Did you ever gamble longer than you had planned?

15. Have you ever gambled to escape worry or trouble?

---

*Reprinted with permission from Gamblers Anonymous. © by Gamblers Anonymous.

16. Have you ever committed, or considered committing, an illegal act to finance gambling?

17. Did gambling cause you to have difficulty in sleeping?

18. Do arguments, disappointments, or frustrations create within you an urge to gamble?

19. Did you ever have an urge to celebrate any good fortune by a few hours of gambling?

20. Have you ever considered self-destruction or suicide, as a result of your gambling?

Most compulsive gamblers will answer yes to at least seven of these questions.

Gam-Anon Family Groups, Inc.
International Service Office
P.O. Box 157
Whitestone, NY 11357
(718) 352-1671
(718) 746-2571

Summary*

These groups are composed of men and women who are husbands, wives, relatives, or close friends of compulsive gamblers. They understand that compulsive gambling is an illness that they cannot control. They are seeking a solution for living with this problem by changing their own lives. This is accomplished by:

1. Spiritual growth through living by the 12 steps of Gam-Anon.

2. Endeavoring to give encouragement and understanding to the compulsive gambler.

3. Welcoming and giving comfort and assistance to the families of compulsive gamblers.

They are made aware that by joining Gam-Anon, they help themselves and ought not join for the purpose of forcing their compulsive gambler into G.A. In truth, it often follows that when the family gains understanding of the problem and attends Gam-Anon faithfully, sooner or later the gambler comes to G.A. This is because the family learns not to enable (help) the gambler, and, because the compulsive gambler sees spiritual principles working which he or she decides these principles can work for them, too. However, families are told not to expect this fortunate result, and that it is important that they come to Gam-Anon to find a new way of life for themselves.

Goal

To not concentrate on the compulsive gambler, but make healthy decisions in their own lives, and to give encouragement and understanding to the compulsive gambler.

Self-Assessment Questions —
Is There a Gambling Problem In Your Family?*

If there is a gambling problem in your home, the Gam-Anon family groups may be able to help you cope with it. If you are living with a compulsive gambler, you will answer yes to at least six of the following questions:

---

*Reprinted with permission from Gam-Anon Family Groups, Inc. © by Gam-Anon Family Groups, Inc.

1. Do you find yourself constantly bothered by bill collectors?

2. Is the person in question often away from home for long, unexplained periods of time?

3. Does this person ever lose time from work due to gambling?

4. Do you feel that this person cannot be trusted with money?

5. Does the person in question faithfully promise that he or she will stop gambling; beg, plead for another chance, yet gamble again and again?

6. Does this person ever gamble longer than he or she intended to, until the last dollar is gone?

7. Does this person immediately return to gambling to try to recover losses, or to win more?

8. Does this person ever gamble to get money to solve financial difficulties, or have unrealistic expectations that gambling will bring the family material comfort and wealth?

9. Does this person borrow money to gamble with or to pay gambling debts?

10. Has this person's reputation ever suffered due to gambling, even to the extent of committing illegal acts to finance gambling?

11. Have you come to the point of hiding money needed for living expenses, knowing that you and the rest of the family may go without food and clothing if you do not?

12. Do you search this person's clothing or go through his or her wallet when the opportunity presents itself, or otherwise check on his or her activities?

13. Do you hide his or her money?

14. Have you noticed a personality change in the gambler as his or her gambling progresses?

15. Does the person in question consistently lie to cover-up or deny his or her gambling activities?

16. Does this person use guilt induction as a method of shifting responsibilities for his or her gambling upon you?

17. Do you attempt to anticipate this person's moods, or try to control his or her life?

18. Does this person ever suffer from remorse or depression due to gambling sometimes to the point of self-destruction?

19. Has the gambling ever brought you to the point of threatening to break up the family unit?

20. Do you feel that your life together is a nightmare?

In Gam-Anon, we learn effective ways of coping with the gambling problem. By seeking help for ourselves and gaining serenity and peace of mind, we find that we are better able to cope with our problems on a day-to-day basis and in some cases motivate the gambler toward seeking help for him or herself.

Helping Cross-Dressers Anonymous (HCDA)
HCDA
6804E Hwy. 6 South #334
Houston, TX 77083
Website: http://www.firstnethou.com/brenda/hcda.htm

Summary*

HCDA groups are fellowships of cross-dressers and those who are affected by cross-dressing, who share their experiences, strength, and hope in order to solve their common problems. They believe cross-dressing is an outward expression of an inner essence of their total being and as such is natural for them. They believe they can find happiness and a productive place in society, not by confrontational behavior or aggressive promotion, but by being positive and productive citizens.

They believe they can contribute positively to our society in general and strive to help one another achieve the highest degree of self-actualization possible under the circumstances of their individual lives.

HCDA has but one purpose, to help cross-dressers. They do this by practicing the 12 steps of HCDA, by welcoming and giving comfort to cross-dressers, and by giving them understanding and encouragement as they grow toward security.

What is Cross-Dressing?*

As the word implies, cross-dressing is wearing clothes (dressing: the act of donning clothing and wearing it). The "cross" comes in when a person goes against the prevailing socially-defined stereotypes, dons and wears clothing society says is exclusively for members of the sex opposite to the sex of the person involved.

HESHE Anonymous (HESHE)
HESHE World Service Office
P.O. Box 1752
Keene, New Hampshire 03431
http://www.berks.com/12step
http://adam.cheshire.net/~troy
http://www.berks.com/heshe

Summary

HESHE Anonymous Preamble:* HESHE Anonymous is a fellowship of men and women who share their progress, feelings, some reflection, and how they live and work the 12 steps, with others that we may solve our common problem and help others to recover from addiction, addictive behavior, and emotional suffering. The only requirement for membership is a desire to recover.

Their primary purpose is to stay mentally and emotionally sober and help others to achieve sobriety. They realize this is a full-circle disease, they remain friendly with the legal, medical, and psychiatric fields to insure that they are not working against each other. They do this through the one combined voice of their group conscience as a whole. Each individual's bottom line sobriety may be different and their problems may be different, but the feelings and struggles mirror their own. They take peoples pain and joy as serious as they take their own. They ask that each member be light and brief on details. Some things are better shared with a sponsor. It is an anonymous program, so please protect whom you see and what you hear. When sharing it is very important that we keep the focus on themselves and please no cross talk.

Incest Survivors Anonymous (I.S.A.)
I.S.A.
P.O. Box 17245
Long Beach, CA 90807-7245
(Self-addressed, stamped envelope)
Email: 66239@lafn.org

Summary*

An international self-help, mutual-help recovery program for men, women, and teens. Based on " . . . God as we understand Him" — Step Three, the 12 Steps, and 12 Traditions of Alcoholics Anonymous adapted to incest with permission of A.A.. World Service New York. Only for and by survivors and their personal prosurvivors. No perpetrators or satanists. No professionals as professionals — only as survivors. No students as students — only as survivors.

I.S.A. short form of the definition of incest is described as: touching and non-touching, verbal and non-verbal, overt and covert. The perpetrator may be known to the victim or may be a stranger.

For I.S.A. meetings, information, and literature, write I.S.A. Please state if you are a survivor, or other status, that we may serve you better. Don't quit before your miracles.

---

*Reprinted with permission from Incest Survivors Anonymous. © by Incest Survivors Anonymous.

Marijuana Anonymous (MA)

P. O. Box 2912

Van Nuys, CA 91404

(800) 766-6779

Website: http://www.marijuana-anonymous.org/

Email: info@marijuana-anonymous.org

Summary*

A fellowship of people of all ages who are addicted or suspect they may be addicted to marijuana.

Goal

To abstain from using marijuana.

Self-Assessment Questions*

1. Has smoking pot stopped being fun?

2. Do you ever get high alone?

3. Is it hard for you to imagine a life without marijuana?

4. Do you find that your friends are determined by your marijuana use?

5. Do you smoke marijuana to avoid dealing with your problems?

6. Do you smoke pot to cope with your feelings?

7. Does your marijuana use let you live in a privately-defined world?

8. Have you ever failed to keep promises you made about cutting down or controlling your dope smoking?

9. Has your use of marijuana caused problems with memory, concentration, or motivation?

10. When your stash is nearly empty, do you feel anxious or worried about how to get more?

11. Do you plan your life around your marijuana use?

12. Have friends or relatives ever complained that your pot smoking is damaging your relationship with them?

If you answered yes to any of the above questions, you may have a problem with marijuana.

---

*Reprinted with permission of the Marijuana Anonymous Public Information Trustee. © by Marijuana Anonymous World Service.

Narcotics Anonymous (NA)
World Service Office, Inc.
P.O. Box 9999
Van Nuys, CA 91409
Tel. (818) 773-9999
Fax (818) 700-0700
Website: http://www.narcotics-anonymous.org/

World Service Office - Europe
48 Rue de l'Ete/Zomerstraat
B-1050 Brussels, Belgium
Tel. 32-2-646-6012
Fax 32-2-649-9239

Summary

A fellowship of people of all ages who are addicted or suspect they are addicted to drugs.

Goal

To abstain from all drugs, including alcohol.

Self-Assessment Questions — Am I an Addict?*

Only you can answer this question. This may not be an easy thing to do. All through our use, we told ourselves, "I can handle it." Even if this was true in the beginning, it is not so now. The drugs handled us. We lived to use and used to live. Very simply, an addict is a person whose life is controlled by drugs.

Perhaps you admit you have a problem with drugs, but you don't consider yourself an addict. All of us have preconceived ideas about what an addict is. There is nothing shameful about being an addict once you begin to take positive action. If you can identify with our problems, you may be able to identify with our solution. The following questions were written by recovering addicts in Narcotics Anonymous. If you have doubts about whether or not you're an addict, take a few moments to read the questions below and answer them as honestly as you can.

1. Do you ever use alone?

2. Have you ever substituted one drug for another, thinking that one particular drug was the problem?

*Reprinted with permission from Narcotics Anonymous World Service Office, Inc. from *Am I an Addict?* © 1986 by Narcotics Anonymous World Service Office, Inc.

3. Have you ever manipulated or lied to a doctor to obtain prescription drugs?

4. Have you ever stolen drugs or stolen to obtain drugs?

5. Do you regularly use a drug when you wake up or when you go to bed?

6. Have you ever taken one drug to overcome the effects of another?

7. Do you avoid people or places that do not approve of you using drugs?

8. Have you ever used a drug without knowing what it was or what it would do to you?

9. Has your job or school performance ever suffered from the effects of your drug use?

10. Have you ever been arrested as a result of using drugs?

11. Have you ever lied about what and how much you use?

12. Do you put the purchase of drugs ahead of your financial responsibilities?

13. Have you ever tried to stop or control your using?

14. Have you ever been in a jail, hospital, or drug rehabilitation center because of your using?

15. Does using interfere with your sleeping or eating?

16. Does the thought of running out of drugs terrify you?

17. Do you feel it is impossible for you to live without drugs?

18. Do you ever question your own sanity?

19. Is your drug use making life at home unhappy?

20. Have you ever thought you couldn't fit in or have a good time without drugs?

21. Have you ever felt defensive, guilty, or ashamed about your using?

22. Do you think a lot about drugs?

23. Have you had irrational or indefinable fears?

24. Has using affected your sexual relationships?

25. Have you ever taken drugs you didn't prefer?

26. Have you ever used drugs because of emotional pain or stress?

27. Have you ever overdosed on any drugs?

28. Do you continue to use despite negative consequences?

29. Do you think you might have a drug problem?

"Am I an addict"? This is a question only you can answer. We found that we all answered different numbers of these questions yes. The actual number of yes responses wasn't as important as how we felt inside and how addiction had affected our lives.

Some of these questions don't even mention drugs. This is because addiction is an insidious disease that affects all areas of our lives — even those areas which seem at first to have little to do with drugs. The different drugs we used were not as important as why we used them and what they did to us.

When we first read these questions, it was frightening for us to think we might be addicts. Some of us tried to dismiss these thoughts by saying: "Oh, those questions don't make sense," or "I'm different. I know I take drugs, but I'm not an addict. I have real emotional, family, and/or job problems," or "I'm just having a rough time getting it together right now," or "I'll be able to stop when I find the right person, get the right job, etc."

Nar-Anon Family Groups Headquarters, Inc.
P.O. Box 2562
Palos Verdes Peninsula, CA 90274
(310) 547-5800

Summary
A fellowship of families and friends of addicts in recovery, or constant relapsers, or still denying that a problem exists.

Goal
To learn how to relinquish trying to control the addict and to make choices for their own lives that will enable them to experience peace and serenity.

Nar-Ateen
c/o Nar-Anon Family Groups Headquarters, Inc.
P.O. Box 2562
Palos Verdes Peninsula, CA 90274
(310) 547-5800

Summary

A program of teen-aged family members and friends of addicts in recovery, or constant relapsers, or still denying that a problem exists.

Goal

To learn and develop coping skills and to learn how to make choices for their own lives that will enable them to experience peace and serenity.

Nar-Atot
c/o Nar-Anon Family Groups Headquarters, Inc.
P.O. Box 2562
Palos Verdes Peninsula, CA 90274
(310) 547-5800

Summary

A program of children, family members, and friends of addicts in recovery, or constant relapsers, or still denying that a problem exists.

Goal

To learn and develop coping skills and to learn how to express their feelings.

Nicotine Anonymous (NA)
World Service Office, Inc.
P.O. Box 126338
Harrisburg, PA 17112-6338
(415) 922-8575
Email: info@nicotine-anonymous.org
Website: http:\\www.nicotine-anonymous.org

Summary

Nicotine Anonymous is a community of people who have felt the grip of nicotine addiction. We have found a solution, a way to live and grow without nicotine, and we share it freely with each other and with anyone that wishes to join us.

We know that nicotine is a subtly powerful mind- and mood-altering substance and that the craving for it can return at any time. Many who have stopped for years have found themselves smoking once more. Therefore, we meet regularly to avoid slipping back into the addiction.

Goal

Live and enjoy life without nicotine.

Self-Assessment Questions*

Answer the following questions as honestly as you can:

1. Do you smoke everyday?

2. Do you smoke because of shyness and to build up self-confidence?

3. Do you smoke to escape from boredom and worries while under pressure?

4. Have you ever burned a hole in your clothes, carpet, furniture, or car?

5. Have you ever had to go to the store late at night or at another inconvenient time because you were out of cigarettes?

6. Do you feel defensive or angry when people tell you that your cigarette smoke is bothering them?

7. Has a doctor or dentist suggested that you stop smoking?

8. Have you promised someone that you would stop smoking, then broken your promise?

9. Have you felt physical or emotional discomfort when trying to quit?

---

*Reprinted with permission from Nicotine Anonymous World Service Office, Inc. © by Nicotine Anonymous World Service Office, Inc.

10. Have you successfully stopped smoking for a period of time only to start again?

11. Do you buy extra supplies of tobacco to make sure you won't run out?

12. Do you find it difficult to imagine life without smoking?

13. Do you choose only activities and entertainment such that you can smoke during them?

14. Do you prefer, seek out, or feel more comfortable in the company of smokers?

15. Do you inwardly despise or feel ashamed of yourself because of your smoking?

16. Do you ever find yourself lighting up without having consciously decided to?

17. Has your smoking caused trouble at home or in a relationship?

18. Do you ever tell yourself that you can stop smoking whenever you want to?

19. Have you ever felt that your life would be better if you didn't smoke?

20. Do you continue to smoke even though you are aware of the health hazards posed by smoking?

If you answered yes to one or two of these questions, there is a chance that you are addicted or are becoming addicted to nicotine. If you answered yes to three or more, you are probably already addicted to nicotine.

Obsessive & Compulsive Anonymous (OCA)
P.O. Box 215
New Hyde Park, NY 11040
(516) 741-4901
Website: http://members.aol.com/west24th/index.html

Summary

A fellowship of people who suffer with obsessive compulsive disorder (OCD), which is characterized by distressing patterns of repetitive thoughts and behaviors. A fellowship of people who share their experience, strength, and hope with each other that they may solve their common problem and help others recover from OCD. The only requirement for membership is a desire to recover from OCD.

Goal

To find freedom from the limitations of living a life controlled by OCD through the 12 steps. Our primary purpose is to recover from OCD and to help others.

What is OCD?*

OCD is characterized by recurrent, unwanted, and unpleasant thoughts (obsessions), and or repetitive, ritualistic behaviors, which the person feels driven to perform (compulsions), people with OCD know their obsessions and compulsions are irrational or excessive, yet find they have little or no control over them.

Typical obsessions include: dirt, germs, contaminations, fear of acting on violent or aggressive impulses, feeling overly responsible for the safety of others, for example, unreasonable fear of having run over someone with a car, abhorrent religious (blasphemous) and sexual thoughts, inordinate concern with order, arrangement, or symmetry, inability to discard useless or worn out possessions, etc.

Typical compulsions include: excessive washing (particularly handwashing or bathing), cleaning, checking and repetitive actions such as touching, counting, arranging and ordering, or hoarding. Ritualistic behaviors lessen the chances of distress from obsessions but only buy short-term comfort at the long-term cost of frequent ritual repetition.

---

*Reprinted with permission of Obsessive & Compulsive Anonymous from *Obsessive Compulsive Anonymous — Recovering from Obsessive Compulsive Disorder.* © 1990 by Obsessive & Compulsive Anonymous.

Overeaters Anonymous, Inc. (OA)
World Service Office
6075 Zenith Court NE
Rio Rancho, NM 87124
(505) 891-2664
Fax: (505) 891-4320
Email: overeatr@technet.nm.org
Website: http:\\www.overeatersanonymous.org

Summary*

A fellowship of people of all ages who share the common disease of compulsive overeating. For weight loss, any medically-approved eating plan is acceptable. The only requirement for membership is a desire to stop eating compulsively. OA is self-supporting through member contributions; there are no dues or fees.

Goal*

To recover from compulsive overeating by approaching the disease on three levels: spiritual, emotional, and physical.

Self-Assessment Questions —
Are You a Compulsive Overeater?**

This series of questions may help you determine if you are a compulsive overeater. Many members of Overeaters Anonymous have found that they have answered yes to many of these questions.

1. Do you eat when you're not hungry?

2. Do you go on eating binges for no apparent reason?

3. Do you have feelings of guilt and remorse after overeating?

4. Do you give too much time and thought to food?

5. Do you look forward with pleasure and anticipation to the moments when you can eat alone?

6. Do you plan these secret binges ahead of time?

7. Do you eat sensibly before others and make up for it alone?

8. Is your weight affecting the way you live your life?

9. Have you tried to diet for a week (or longer), only to fall short of your goal?

---

*Reprinted with permission of Overeaters Anonymous, Inc.. © Overeaters Anonymous, Inc.
**Reprinted with permission of Overeaters Anonymous, Inc. from *Fifteen Questions*. © 1986 by Overeaters Anonymous, Inc.

10. Do you resent others telling you to "use a little willpower" to stop overeating?

11. Despite evidence to the contrary, have you continued to assert that you can diet "on your own" whenever you wish?

12. Do you crave food at a definite time, day or night, other than mealtimes?

13. Do you eat to escape from worries or trouble?

14. Have you ever been treated for obesity or a food-related condition?

15. Does your eating behavior make you or others unhappy?

O-Anon Family Groups, Inc.
General Service Office
P.O. Box 748
San Pedro, CA 90733
Telephone and Fax: (310) 547-1570

Summary

A fellowship of relatives and friends of compulsive overeaters.

Goal*

To offer comfort, hope, and friendship; to give understanding and encouragement to the compulsive overeater; and to learn to use the 12 steps as tools for spiritual growth.

Partners and Friends of Incest Survivors Anonymous (PFISA)
c/o Incest Survivors Anonymous (I.S.A.)
P.O. Box 17245
Long Beach, CA 90807-7245
(Enclose self-addressed stamped envelope)
Website: http://www.cs.utk.edu/~bartley/other/pfisa.html

Summary*

Partners and Friends of Incest Survivors Anonymous is a 12-step fellowship open to women and men. The 12-step program is a program of healing for partners of survivors, ex-partners of survivors, partners who are also survivors, friends of survivors, and concerned family members who have a survivor as a relative.

Partners and Friends of Incest Survivors Anonymous is a place where people can talk with someone who understands as perhaps others cannot about the impact of sexual abuse on families and intimate relationships.

---

*Reprinted with permission of Incest Survivors Anonymous from Partners and Friends of Incest Survivors Anonymous website.

Pills Anonymous (PA)
P.O. Box 1031
New York, NY 10028
(212) 874-0700

Summary*

A fellowship of people who are addicted or suspect they are addicted to pills or any mind-altering chemicals.

Goal*

To abstain from pills and any mind-altering chemicals. Recover one day at a time by sharing their experience, strengths, and hopes with each other.

Phobics Anonymous (PA)
World Service Office
P.O. Box 1180
Palm Springs, CA 92263

Summary

Founded 1985. Phobics Anonymous is a 12-step program for people with anxiety and panic disorders.

Goal

To be free from the limitations of the phobia(s).

Recoveries Anonymous (RA)
Universal Services
P.O. Box 1212
East Northport, NY 11731-0558
Telephone: (516) 261-1212
Website: http://www.R-A.org

Summary*

Recoveries Anonymous is a fellowship formed to offer anyone, with any self-destructive or dysfunctional problem, a program of recovery through the 12 Steps, 12 Traditions, and 12 Concepts that were originated by the founders of Alcoholics Anonymous and are now distinctively applied in R.A.'s 12 Ideals. Our experience is that the original spiritual program, which led thousands of alcoholics to recover from their self-destructive behavior and attitudes, can also be applied, by anyone, to any other symptom, such as a compulsive eating disorder, compulsive gambling, compulsive spending, compulsive sexual behavior, emotional extremes, drug addiction, smoking, etc.

Recoveries Anonymous came into existence to serve the need of those who had attended one or more of the many 12-step programs, but despite their best efforts, could not find the recovery they were looking for. It is also for those who may have found some recovery, yet have been frustrated by the endless discussion of, and focus upon, personal problems and self-destructive behavior. While many of these people have stopped self-destructing, they feel that something is still missing from their lives, their program, and their recovery.

In addition, since we do not usually discuss personal problems at R.A. meetings, family and friends are also welcome, even encouraged, to fully participate in every aspect of our program. Experience has shown that there are many benefits when family and friends have the option of joining in the practice of our program, and of attending our meetings. They often benefit from working our program in their own lives.

You can contact Recoveries Anonymous and download a free copy of R.A.'s Newcomer Guide by visiting our website located at http://www.R-A.org.

You can add your name to our mailing list and have us send you a copy of our Newcomer Guide, or information about how to start an R.A. group, by regular mail, if you email us your name and address using the form on our website.

You can also contact Recoveries Anonymous by calling our computerized information and message system. This service can be reached by dialing 1-516-261-1212 from a touch-tone phone. This service is available 24 hours a day, seven days a week.

---

*Reprinted with permission of R.A. Universal Services, Inc. ©1998 by R.A. Universal Services, Inc.

By following the recorded instructions, you can receive detailed information about our fellowship. You can add your name to our mailing list so you can receive our newsletter and announcements. You can request information about how to start an R.A. group, and more.

Recovering Couples Anonymous (RCA)
World Service Organization
P.O. Box 11872
St. Louis, MO 63105
Telephone: (314) 397-0867
Fax: (314) 397-1319
Email: rcawso@aol.com
Website: http://www.recovering-couples.org

Summary

Sometimes this group is open to all 12-step fellowship issues, and sometimes it is closed to sexual issues. Ask about the purpose of the local group.

Characteristics of Functional and Dysfunctional Couples*

1. **Dysfunctional:** Being together and unhappy is safer than being alone.

    Functional: Being together brings us joy and happiness.

2. **Dysfunctional:** It is safer to be with other people than it is to be alone and intimate with our partner.

    Functional: Being alone and intimate with our partner is as safe as being with other people.

3. **Dysfunctional:** If I really let my partner know what I've done or what I'm feeling and thinking (who I am), she or he will leave me.

    Functional: When I really let my partner know what I've done or what I'm thinking (who I am), it increases our intimacy. It's met with acceptance.

4. **Dysfunctional:** It is easier to hide (medicate) our feelings through addictive/compulsive behavior than it is to express them.

    Functional: We no longer need to hide and medicate our feelings through our addictive/compulsive behavior. We can express our feelings.

5. **Dysfunctional:** Being enmeshed and totally dependent with each other is perceived as being in love.

    Functional: Being interdependent adds strength to the relationship.

6. **Dysfunctional:** We find it difficult to ask for what we need, both individually and as a couple.

    Functional: We are learning to ask for what we need, both individually and a couple.

---

7. **Dysfunctional:** Being sexual is equal to being intimate.

   Functional: Being sexual enhances our relationship (increases our intimacy).

8. **Dysfunctional:** We either avoid our problems or feel we are individually responsible for solving the problems we have as a couple.

   Functional: We are learning to face our problems and not to feel individually responsible for solving the problems we have as a couple.

9. **Dysfunctional:** We believe that we must agree on everything.

   Functional: We believe we don't have to agree on everything.

10. **Dysfunctional:** We believe that we must enjoy the same things and have the same interests.

    Functional: We believe we can have different interests and enjoy different things and enjoy being together.

11. **Dysfunctional:** We believe that to be a good couple we must be socially acceptable.

    Functional: We don't have to be socially acceptable.

12. **Dysfunctional:** We have forgotten how to play together.

    Functional: We can play and have fun together.

13. **Dysfunctional:** It is safer to get upset about little issues than to express our true feelings about larger ones.

    Functional: We are learning to express our true feelings about larger issues, and we are learning to resolve conflict.

14. **Dysfunctional:** It is easier to blame our partners than it is to accept our own responsibility.

    Functional: We are learning to accept our individual responsibility.

15. **Dysfunctional:** We deal with conflict by getting totally out of control or by not arguing at all.

    Functional: We are learning to deal with conflict and to fight fairly.

16. **Dysfunctional:** We experience ourselves as inadequate parents.

    Functional: We accept our limitations as parents.

17. **Dysfunctional:** We are ashamed of ourselves as a couple.

    Functional: We are proud of ourselves as a couple.

18. **Dysfunctional:** We repeat patterns of dysfunction from our families-of-origin.

    Functional: We are recognizing and breaking the patterns of dysfunction from our families-of-origin.

Relationships Anonymous (RA)
Website: http://www.geocities.com/HotSprings/Spa/2700/
Email: SUZN222222@aol.com

Summary*

A fellowship that is open to anyone as long as he or she is committed to building healthier relationships. Some of us are trying to improve our current relationships with spouses or lovers, some of us are trying to find the support to end unhealthy relationships, others are not involved with anyone and are working on building self-esteem and awareness of how to improve future relationships. Some of us have been in a series of destructive relationships; others have systematically avoided involvement, fearing hurt or abandonment. But all of us realize the responsibility is ours to build successful and rewarding relationships, and we are committed in our efforts.

Although we focus on intimate relationships, relationships with parents, children, friends, or even co-workers can also be addictive. An addictive relationship is one in which we rely on someone to fulfill our unmet needs from childhood, to escape our own inner sadness, turmoil and pain, to heal us and "save" us through their attention and love, and to make us feel "whole." Ironically, we try to gain control of our lives by giving control to others, and manipulating them to take care of us and solve our problems. We may feel a sense of not being good enough, mixed with a perception of never receiving enough.

Goal

To break the pattern of destructive and addictive relationships. The only requirement for R.A. membership is a desire to have healthier relationships.

---

*Reprinted with permission of Relationships Anonymous. © 1986 Brenda Schaeffer.

Self-Mutilators Anonymous (SMA)
c/o S. Goldberg
129 Pacific Street
Brooklyn, NY 11201

Summary*

Self-Mutilators Anonymous is a fellowship of men and women who share their experience, strength, and hope with each other, that they may solve their common problems and help others recover from physical self-mutilation. SMA provides mutual support and information to people who injure themselves internally or externally.

Goal*

To stop the mutilating behavior and help others recover through practical application of the 12 steps, self-disclosure, and honesty, as well as through the stories of how people have recovered from self-injury.

---

*Reprinted with permission of Shelly Goldberg, founder, Self-Mutilators Anonymous. © Self-Mutilators Anonymous.

Sex Addicts Anonymous (S.A.A.)
International Service Office of S.A.A.
P.O. Box 70949
Houston, TX 77270
(713) 869-4902
Website: http://www.saa-recovery.org
And http://www.sexaa.org/
email: info@saa-recovery.org

Summary

A fellowship of men and women who share their experience, strength, and hope with each other and work the 12-step program of S.A.A. in order to stop their addictive sexual behavior.

Goal

To stop the compulsive sexual behavior.

A Useful Tool for Self-Assessment*

Answer these 12 questions to assess whether you may have a problem with sexual addiction.

1. Do you keep secrets about your sexual or romantic activities from those important to you? Do you lead a double life?

2. Have your needs driven you to have sex in places or situations or with people you would not normally choose?

3. Do you find yourself looking for sexually-arousing articles or scenes in newspapers, magazines, or other media?

4. Do you find that romantic or sexual fantasies interfere with your relationships or are preventing you from facing problems?

5. Do you frequently want to get away from a sex partner after having sex? Do you frequently feel remorse, shame, or guilt after a sexual encounter?

6. Do you feel shame about your body or your sexuality, such that you avoid touching your body or engaging in sexual relationships? Do you fear that you have no sexual feelings, that you are asexual?

7. Does each new relationship continue to have the same destructive patterns which prompted you to leave the last relationship?

---

*Reprinted with permission of Sex Addicts Anonymous World Service, Inc. from *Sex Addicts Anonymous*. ©1997 by Sex Addicts Anonymous World Service, Inc.

8. Is it taking more variety and frequency of sexual and romantic activities than previously to bring the same levels of excitement and relief?

9. Have you been arrested or are you in danger of being arrested because of your practices of voyeurism, exhibitionism, prostitution, sex with minors, indecent phone calls, etc.?

10. Does your pursuit of sex or romantic relationships interfere with your spiritual beliefs or development?

11. Do your sexual activities include the risk, threat or reality of disease, pregnancy, coercion, or violence?

12. Has your sexual or romantic behavior ever left you feeling hopeless, alienated from others, or suicidal?

If you answered yes to more than one of these questions, we would encourage you to seek out additional literature as a resource or to attend a Sex Addicts Anonymous meeting to further assess your needs.

Sex and Love Addicts Anonymous (SLAA)
The Augustine Fellowship
P.O. Box 338
Norwood, MA 02062
(781) 255-8825
Website: HTTP://WWW.SLAAFWS.ORG
Email: slaafws@aol.com

Summary — The Sex and Love Addicts Anonymous Preamble*

Sex and Love Addicts Anonymous is a Twelve Step, Twelve Tradition-oriented fellowship based on the model pioneered by Alcoholics Anonymous.

The only qualification for S.L.A.A. membership is a desire to stop living out a pattern of sex and love addiction. S.L.A.A. is supported entirely through contributions of its membership, and is free to all who need it.

To counter the destructive consequences of sex and love addiction we draw on four major resources:

1. our willingness to stop acting out in our own personal bottom line addictive behavior on a daily basis.

2. our capacity to reach out for the supportive fellowship with S.L.A.A.

3. our practice of the Twelve Step program of recovery to achieve sexual and emotional sobriety.

4. our developing a relationship with a Power greater than ourselves which can guide and sustain us in recovery.

As a fellowship S.L.A.A. has no opinion on outside issues and seeks no controversy. S.L.A.A. is not affiliated with any other organizations, movements or causes, either religious or secular.

We are, however, united in a common focus: dealing with our addictive sexual and emotional behavior. We find a *common denominator* in our obsessive/compulsive patterns which renders any personal differences of sexual or gender orientation irrelevant.

We need to protect with special care the anonymity of every S.L.A.A. member. Additionally, we try to avoid drawing undue attention to S.L.A.A. as a whole from the public media.

---

*Reprinted with permission of The Augustine Fellowship, Fellowship-Wide Services, Inc. from *Basic Text of Sex and Love Addicts Anonymous.* ©1986 by The Augustine Fellowship, Fellowship-Wide Services, Inc.

Sexaholics Anonymous (SA)
SA International Central Office
P.O. Box 111910
Nashville, TN 37222
615-331-6230; Fax: 615-331-6901; 9 a.m. - 5 p.m., M - F
Email: saico@sa.org
Website: http://www.sa.org
Intake procedures: Call, email, or write the Central Office.

Summary*
Formed in 1976. An international organization offering a recovery program based on A.A.'s 12 steps for those who want to stop their sexually self-destructive thinking and behavior. The only requirement for membership is a desire to stop lusting and become sexually sober.

Self-Assessment Questions*
1. Have you ever thought you needed help for your sexual thinking or behavior?
2. That you'd be better off if you didn't keep "giving in"?
3. That sex or stimuli are controlling you?
4. Have you ever tried to stop or limit doing what you felt was wrong in your sexual behavior?
5. Do you resort to sex to escape, relieve anxiety, or because you can't cope?
6. Do you feel guilt, remorse, or depression afterward?
7. Has your pursuit of sex become more compulsive?
8. Does it interfere with relations with your spouse?
9. Do you have to resort to images or memories during sex?
10. Does an irresistible impulse arise when the other party makes the overtures or sex is offered?
11. Do you keep going from one "relationship" or lover to another?
12. Do you feel the "right relationship" would help you stop lusting, masturbating, or being so promiscuous?
13. Do you have a destructive need — a desperate sexual or emotional need for someone?
14. Does pursuit of sex make you careless for yourself or the welfare of your family or others?

---

*Reprinted with permission of Sexaholics Anonymous. © 1985 by Sexaholics Anonymous. Permission to reprint does not imply SA affiliation or SA's review or endorsement of this publication.

15. Has your effectiveness or concentration decreased as sex has become more compulsive?

16. Do you lose time from work for it?

17. Do you turn to a lower environment when pursuing sex?

18. Do you want to get away from the sex partner as soon as possible after the act?

19. Although your spouse is sexually compatible, do you still masturbate or have sex with others?

20. Have you ever been arrested for a sex-related offense?

S-Anon International Family Groups, Inc.
P.O. Box 111242
Nashville, TN 37222-1242
(615) 833-3152
Website: http://www.sanon.org/
Email: sanon@sanon.org

Summary*

S-Anon is a fellowship of people who share their experience, strength, and hope with each other so that they may solve their common problems and help others to recover. The only requirement for membership is that there be a problem of sexaholism in a relative or friend. There are no dues or fees for S-Anon membership; we are self-supporting through our own contributions. S-Anon is not allied with any sect, denomination, politics, organization, or institution, does not wish to engage in any controversy; neither endorses nor opposes any causes. Our primary purpose is to recover from the effects on us of another person's sexaholism, and to help families and friends of sexaholics.

Self-Assessment Questions — The S-Anon Checklist*

1. Have you often felt hurt, ashamed, or embarrassed by someone else's sexual conduct?

2. Are you afraid to upset the sexaholic for fear that he or she will leave you?

3. Have you sometimes found yourself searching for clues about someone else's sexual behavior?

4. Have you ever fantasized, obsessed, or worried about someone else's sexual problem?

5. Have you every made threats to others or promises to yourself ("If this happens again, I'll leave") that you did not carry out?

6. Have you ever tried to control somebody else's sexual thoughts or behavior by doing things like throwing away pornography, dressing suggestively, or being sexual with them in order to keep them from being sexual with others?

7. Has your involvement with another person or their sexual behavior ever affected your relationship with your children, your co-workers, or other friends or family members?

---

8. Have you often lied to others or made excuses to yourself about another person's sexual conduct?

9. Have you had money problems because of someone else's sexual behavior?

10. Have you engaged in sexual behavior that makes you feel uncomfortable or ashamed, or is physically dangerous, fearing that if you don't the sexaholic will leave you?

11. Have you ever felt confused and unable to separate what is true from what is not true when talking with the sexaholic?

12. Have you ever thought about or attempted suicide because of someone else's sexual behavior?

13. Have you often used sex in order to have peace in the family or smooth over problems?

14. Does sex (for example, thinking about it, doing it, talking about it, worrying about it) play an all-consuming role in the relationship?

15. Have you ever felt abandoned emotionally because of your partner's use of pornography or masturbation?

16. Have you ever helped someone get out of jail or other legal trouble as a result of his or her sexual behavior or feared that this kind of thing could happen?

17. Have you often thought that the sexaholic's behavior was caused by other people, such as friends or sexual partners? by society in general? by his/her job, religion, or birth family?

18. Have you ever suspected that anyone was inappropriately sexually interested in any of your children?

19. Do you feel alone in your problem?

If you can answer yes to even some of these questions, you may find help in S-Anon.

Sexual Assault Recovery Anonymous (SARA)
P.O. Box 16
Surrey, British Columbia, Canada V3T 4W4
(604) 584-2626
Fax: (604) 584-2888

Summary
A fellowship providing education and self-help for adults and adolescents who were sexually abused in childhood.

Goal
To find hope and to recover from the damage incurred by the sexual abuse whether or not it occurred once or many times.

Who Does SARA Help?*
- Victims of childhood sexual abuse who are ready to work towards recovery.
- Supportive family members of victims of childhood sexual abuse.

How Do I know SARA is for Me?*
- You are weary from trying to block out the memories of the abuse.
- You want to rid yourself of escape mechanisms (behaviors that allow you not to think).
- You want to learn to accept and face the memories when they do surface; then put them in the past, in a positive way, along with your good memories.

What Age Groups Are Served by SARA?*
The age range for adolescent groups is 13 through 18 years. These suggested guideline for adult groups is age 19 or older. Occasionally SARA runs a group for preteens, aged six to 12 years, but this is dependent upon the availability of trained leaders.

Are There Different Types of Groups?*
Only as far as these classifications go:
- Adult female groups
- Adult male groups
- Teen female groups

---

*Reprinted with permission of Sexual Assault Recovery Anonymous. © 1985 by Sexual Assault Recovery Anonymous.

- Family groups
- Occasionally, a co-ed group

Sexual Compulsives Anonymous (SCA)
P.O. Box 1585 Old Chelsea Station
New York, NY 10011
(212) 606-3778
(800) 977-4325
Website: http://www.sca-recovery.org
Email to: info@sca-recovery.org

Summary*

SCA is a 12-step fellowship, inclusive of all sexual orientations, open to anyone with a desire to recover from sexual compulsion. We are not group therapy, but a spiritual program that provides a safe environment for working on problems of sexual addiction and sexual sobriety.

We believe we are not meant to repress our God-given sexuality, but to learn how to express it in ways that will not make unreasonable demands on our time and energy, place us in legal jeopardy, or endanger our mental, physical, or spiritual health. Members are encouraged to develop a sexual-recovery plan, defining sexual sobriety for themselves.

There are no requirements for admission to our meetings, anyone having difficulties with sexual compulsion is welcome.

Self-Assessment Questions*

1. Do you frequently experience remorse, depression, or guilt about your sexual activity?

2. Do you feel your sexual drive and activity is getting out of control? Have you repeatedly tried to stop or reduce certain sexual behaviors, but inevitably you could not?

3. Are you unable to resist sexual advances, or turn down sexual propositions when offered?

4. Do you use sex to escape from uncomfortable feelings such as anxiety, fear, anger, resentment, guilt, etc. which seem to disappear when the sexual obsession starts?

5. Do you spend excessive time obsessing about sex or engaged in sexual activity?

6. Have you neglected your family, friends, spouse, or relationship because of the time you spend in sexual activity?

7. Do your sexual pursuits interfere with your work or professional development?

---

*Reprinted with permission of Sexual Compulsives Anonymous International Service Organization. © 1997 by Sexual Compulsives Anonymous International Service Organization.

8. Is your sexual life secretive, a source of shame, and not in keeping with your values? Do you lie to others to cover up your sexual activity?

9. Are you afraid of sex? Do you avoid romantic and sexual relationships with others and restrict your sexual activity to fantasy, masturbation, and solitary or anonymous activity?

10. Are you increasingly unable to perform sexually without other stimuli such as pornography, videos, "poppers," drugs/alcohol, "toys," etc.?

11. Do you have to resort increasingly to abusive, humiliating, or painful sexual fantasies or behaviors to get sexually aroused?

12. Has your sexual activity prevented you from developing a close, loving relationship with a partner? Or, have you developed a pattern of intense romantic or sexual relationships that never seem to last once the excitement wears off?

13. Do you only have anonymous sex or one-night stands? Do you usually want to get away from your sexual partner after the encounter?

14. Do you have sex with people with whom you normally would not associate?

15. Do you frequent clubs, bars, adult bookstores, restrooms, parks, and other public places in search of sexual partners?

16. Have you ever been arrested or placed yourself in legal jeopardy for your sexual activity?

17. Have you ever risked your physical health with exposure to sexually-transmitted diseases by engaging in "unsafe" sexual activity?

18. Has the money you spent on pornography, videos, phone sex, or hustlers/prostitutes strained your financial resources?

19. Have people you trust expressed concern about your sexual activity?

20. Does life seem meaningless and hopeless without a romantic or sexual relationship?

These Are the Characteristics
Most of Us Seem to Have in Common*

1. As adolescents, we used fantasy and compulsive masturbation to avoid feelings, and continued this tendency into our adult lives with compulsive sex.

2. Compulsive sex became a drug, which we used to escape from feelings such as anxiety, loneliness, anger, and self-hatred, as well as joy.

3. We tended to become immobilized by romantic obsessions. We became addicted to the search for sex and love; as a result, we neglected our lives.

---

*Reprinted with permission of Sexual Compulsives Anonymous International Service Organization. © 1997 by Sexual Compulsives Anonymous International Service Organization.

4. We sought oblivion in fantasy and masturbation, and lost ourselves in compulsive sex. Sex became a reward, punishment, distraction, and time-killer.

5. Because of our low self-esteem, we used sex to feel validated and complete.

6. We tried to bring intensity and excitement into our lives through sex, but felt ourselves growing steadily emptier.

7. Sex was compartmentalized instead of integrated into our lives as a healthy element.

8. We became addicted to people, and were unable to distinguish among sex, love, and affection.

9. We searched for some "magical" quality in others to make us feel complete. Other people were idealized and endowed with a powerful symbolism, which often disappeared after we had sex with them.

10. We were drawn to people who were not available to us, or who would reject or abuse us.

11. We feared relationships, but continually searched for them. In a relationship, we feared abandonment and rejection, but out of one, we felt empty and incomplete.

12. While constantly seeking intimacy with another person, we found that the desperate quality of our need made true intimacy with anyone impossible, and we often developed unhealthy dependency relationships that eventually became unbearable.

13. Even when we got the love of another person, it never seemed enough, and we were unable to stop lusting after others.

14. Trying to conceal our dependency demands, we grew more isolated from ourselves, from God, and from the very people we longed to be close to.

Sexual Recovery Anonymous (SRA)
P.O. Box 73, Planetarium Station
New York, NY 10024
212-340-4650

P.O. Box 72044
Burnaby, BC V5H 4PQ
CANADA
(606) 290-9382

Summary*

The primary purpose of this 12-step program is to stay sexually sober and help others achieve sobriety. Sobriety is the release from all compulsive and destructive sexual behaviors. They have found through their experience that sobriety includes freedom from masturbation and sex outside a mutually-committed relationship. They believe that spirituality and self-love are antidotes to the addiction. They are walking towards a healthy sexuality. The only requirement for membership is a desire to stop compulsive sexual behavior.

Sex had become a mood-altering behavior to which we turned in order to avoid our true feelings and emotions. This use of sex and sexual fantasy became compulsive; the need to escape, no matter what the cost, was greater than our ability to stop. The "high" we got from sex was so intense that we repeatedly used it in an attempt to avoid the realities of our lives. The pursuit of sex, sexual fantasy, and sexual acting out came to dominate ever greater parts of our existence. We found that no matter how hard we tried to stop or control our behavior, we could not.*

Self-Assessment Questions — Do I belong in SRA?**

The following are a series of statements from SRA members that describe their feelings and behaviors about the addiction. Do these statements apply to you? Check yes or no. Be honest with yourself.

Yes No

☐   ☐   I think about sex or romantic relationships most of the time.

☐   ☐   I often feel shame, regret, or remorse after sexual fantasy or behavior.

☐   ☐   I want to stop masturbating but I can't.

☐   ☐   I have difficulty staying monogamous in a relationship.

Yes	No	
☐	☐	I break promises to myself to stop my unwanted sexual behavior.
☐	☐	My sexual behavior isolates me from my friends, family, etc.
☐	☐	My obsession with pornography interferes with my real relationships.
☐	☐	I obsessively sexualize people on the street.
☐	☐	I put myself at risk of sexually-transmitted diseases.
☐	☐	I've been afraid of my "double life" and sexual secrets being discovered.
☐	☐	I've spent a great deal of time or money on sex.
☐	☐	I have felt compelled to seek new sexual or romantic highs.
☐	☐	My sexual behavior has put me in dangerous situations.
☐	☐	I have hurt myself or others as a result of my sexual behavior.
☐	☐	I have engaged in any of the following: voyeurism, exhibitionism, anonymous sex, phone sex, trading for sex, paying for or being paid for sex, abusive sex.
☐	☐	I have been unable to say no to other people's sexual advances.
☐	☐	I have risked or lost my job because of my sexual behavior.
☐	☐	I feel empty when not in a sexual or romantic relationship.
☐	☐	I feel sex is my most important need.
☐	☐	I am obsessed with romantic possibilities.
☐	☐	I flirt even when I don't mean to.
☐	☐	I obsess about a specific person or act even though it may be painful.
☐	☐	I confuse sex with love.
☐	☐	My sexual behavior has made my life unmanageable.

Sex addiction is a self-diagnosed disease. The above statements are an aid to help you to decide if you are addicted. If you have related to any of these statements, SRA may be a place where you can find help. You are not alone.

Shoplifters Anonymous (SLA)
P.O. Box 24515
Minneapolis, MN 55424
Telephone: (612) 925-4860
Email: tobbit@juno.com

Summary*

A fellowship of people who have a desire to abstain from shoplifting.

Goal

To stop shoplifting (stealing), learn how to live a full life free of this addiction.

Consequences of Shoplifting*

Low self-esteem, general paranoia, and loss of personal freedom, shame, public knowledge, and isolation. All of this can lead to a final destination of jail time. Shoplifters Anonymous groups offer a non-judgmental place to share your story, with offers of help and advice from others that have experienced the same addiction. Currently there are a small number of active groups in the United States, with a great need for more groups. If you are interested in starting a group, or for information and resources about shoplifting, please write or email.

*Reprinted with permission of Shoplifters Anonymous. © 1998 by Shoplifters Anonymous.

Suiciders Anonymous, Inc. (SA)
c/o Maryland Suiciders Anonymous
P.O. Box 3504
Baltimore, MD 21214
Administration Office (410) 426-4357
Grass Roots, Counseling Line (24 hours a day): (800) 422-0009; (410) 531-6677;
(410) 531-5086 (TTY)

Summary*

A program of men and women who share with each other their experiences, strengths, hopes, and faiths in an attempt to solve their common problems and to help others to recover from the depths that lead to thoughts of, or attempts at suicide. S.A. is not a religious organization, but it is spiritual. It is not the only solution — it doesn't work just because a person has a problem — but it does work for those who have a problem and are honest, open, and willing to work the "program."

Basically, it's a 12-step, self-help, support group that offers anonymity along with total acceptance, unconditional and unselfish love. "Agape-Love" — to build a new hope for today, tomorrow, and forever.

Goal

To discover new hope for today, and to help others who have attempted suicide or who have had deep depression which leads to suicidal thoughts. The only requirement for membership is an honest desire to recover from hopelessness and maintain a new hope for today.

---

*Reprinted with permission of Suiciders Anonymous. © by Suiciders Anonymous. Permission to reprint does not imply Suiciders Anonymous affiliation or Suiciders Anonymous' review or endorsement of this publication.

Survivors of Incest Anonymous (SIA)
P.O. Box 21817
Baltimore, MD 21222-6817
(410) 282-3400

Summary

A fellowship of men and women who have been victims of child sexual abuse. SIA provides support groups throughout the world.

Goal

"To find hope and recovery from the damage incurred by the sexual abuse whether it occurred once or many times." (member who wishes to remain anonymous).

Survivors of a Loved One's Suicide Anonymous (SLOSA)
c/o J. Mason
350 West 55 Street
New York, NY 10019
Telephone: (212) 246-3117

Summary

A fellowship of people who have lost loved ones to suicide.

Goal

"Together, deal with the grief, anger, and the void that is left when a loved one takes his or her own life. Recover from this very different kind of death." (J. Mason).

Trauma Survivors Anonymous (TSA)
c/o J. Mason
350 West 55 Street
New York, NY 10019
Telephone: (212) 246-3117

Summary

A fellowship of people who have been wounded by any kind of emotional and/or physical trauma.

Goal

Together, recover from the wounds left by any kind of trauma.

Workaholics Anonymous (WA)
World Service Organization, Inc.
P.O. Box 289
Menlo Park, CA 94026-0289
(510) 273-9253

Summary

A fellowship of individuals who share their experience, strength, and hope with each other that they may solve their common problem and help others to recover from workaholism. The only requirement for membership is the desire to stop working compulsively.

Purpose

Our primary purpose is to stop working compulsively and to carry the message of recovery to workaholics who still suffer.

Self-Assessment Questions —
How Do I Know If I'm a Workaholic?*

1. Do you get more excited about your work than about family or anything else?

2. Are there times when you can charge through your work and other times when you can't get anything done?

3. Do you take work with you to bed? on weekends? on vacation?

4. Is work the activity you like to do best and talk about most?

5. Do you work more than 40 hours a week?

6. Do you turn your hobbies into money-making ventures?

7. Do you take complete responsibility for the outcome of your work efforts?

8. Have your family or friends given up expecting you on time?

9. Do you take on extra work because you are concerned that it won't otherwise get done?

10. Do you underestimate how long a project will take and then rush to complete it?

11. Do you believe that it is okay to work long hours if you love what you are doing?

12. Do you get impatient with people who have other priorities besides work?

13. Are you afraid that if you don't work hard you will lose your job or be a failure?

---

14. Is the future a constant worry for you even when things are going very well?

15. Do you do things energetically and competitively including play?

16. Do you get irritated when people ask you to stop doing your work in order to do something else?

17. Have your long hours hurt your family or other relationships?

18. Do you think about your work while driving, falling asleep, or when others are talking?

19. Do you work or read during meals?

20. Do you believe that more money will solve the other problems in your life?

If you answered yes to three or more of these questions, there is a chance you are a workaholic or well on your way to becoming one.

Work-Anon Family Groups
World Service Organization
P.O. Box 289
Menlo Park, CA 94026-0289
(510) 273-9253

Summary

A fellowship of relatives and friends of people who work compulsively.

Goal

To surrender trying to control the workaholic and deal with the impact the addiction has had on their own lives.

Other Types of Step-Fellowship Programs

Overcomers Outreach, Inc.
520 N. Brookhurst
Suite 121
Anaheim, CA 92801
Telephone: 1-800-310-3001
Telephone in CA: (714) 491-3000
Fax: (714) 491-3004
Email: info@oo.sheperd.com

In Canada: Overcomers Canada
Email: overcomer@mb.imag.net

Summary

A program of men and women who have been affected either directly or indirectly by the abuse of any mood-altering chemical or compulsive behavior. They strongly believe that their "higher Power" is Jesus Christ.

Goals

- To provide fellowship in recovery.
- To be and to live reconciled to God and His family.
- To gain a better understanding of alcohol and other mood-altering substances and the disease of addiction/compulsion.
- To be built up and strengthen in faith in Christ Jesus
- To render dedicated service to others who are suffering as they once suffered.

Homosexuals Anonymous (H.A.)
P.O. Box 7881
Reading, PA 19603 USA
Telephone: 1-610-376-1146
Website: http://members.aol.com/Hawebpage

Summary*

Homosexuals Anonymous (H.A.) is a Christian fellowship of men and women who have chosen to help each other to live free from homosexuality. The purpose of H.A. is to support individuals seeking that freedom. Group support is available through weekly H.A. meetings. Guidance is received through the shared experiences and growth of others. Strength is acquired by training the faith response through the 14 steps.

H.A. is non-sectarian and works inter- and nondenominationally.

H.A. does not endorse or oppose any political causes. It is **not** a crusade against "gay" organizations or movements. It does not wish to engage in any controversial issues that would draw members' energies away from the goal of maturing in their relationships with those around them and rediscovering their true identity through a restored relationship with God through Jesus Christ.

Statement of Philosophy*

Homosexuals Anonymous, a Christian fellowship, holds the view that homosexual activity is not in harmony with the will of God and that the universal creation norm is heterosexuality. Nevertheless, the great message of righteousness by faith in Christ brings mercy and hope to all people in homosexuality.

Christ, the Imago Dei (the Image of God), is the restoration of the creation image, in whom all men and women find their identity by faith. The search for wholeness and heterosexuality within ourselves thus comes to an end. Men and women receive Christ as their image of God, in whom is their wholeness and heterosexuality. As a trained faith grasps this awareness, there is a breaking of the power of the homosexual inclination so that freedom from the homosexual drive and activity is a real possibility.

H.A., however, does **not** believe that a change in homosexual inclination is a requirement for acceptance with God or entrance into the fellowship of the church. Although deliverance from homosexual activity is the call of God, the healing of the homosexual inclination will vary according to growth and is a result of our faith identity with Christ, rather than as a way to it. Nevertheless, H.A. holds that the homosexual inclination may be healed and that all who desire it may realize their inborn, though fallen, heterosexuality, thus opening the way to heterosexual marriage and family.

Parents Anonymous (PA)
Parents Anonymous National Office, Inc.
675 W. Foothill Blvd., Suite 200
Claremont, CA 91711-3745
Telephone: (909) 625-6184 (8 a.m. - 4:30 p.m., M - F)
Fax: (909) 625-6304
Email: parentsanon@msn.com
Website: http://www.parentsanonymous-natl.org/

Canada: PA/Calgary
Ste. 220, 665-8 St. S.W.
Calgary, AB Canada
T2P 3K7
403/263-6663
403/265-1117 (24-hr. stress line)

Summary

Mutual support Parents Anonymous groups available to any parent feeling stress in parenting. Not a 12-step group.

- Service Sites: 1-800-339-6993 (Info. Line); 24 hours/7 days - Los Angeles residents call for information.
- Area Served: National
- Fees: Free Services
- Intake Procedures: Call for information.
- Client Contact: Staff
- Professional Contact: Dr. Luisa Pion-Berlin, National Executive Director
- Special Items: Spanish

Secular Organizations for Sobriety (SOS)
SOS National Clearinghouse
5521 Grosvenor Boulevard
Los Angeles, CA 90066
Telephone: (310) 821-8430
Fax: (310) 821-2610
Email: sosla@loop.com
Website: http://www.unhooked.com

Summary*

An alternative recovery method for those alcoholics or drug addicts who are uncomfortable with the spiritual content of widely available 12-step programs. SOS takes a reasonable, secular approach to recovery and maintains that sobriety is a separate issue from religion or spirituality. SOS credits the individual for achieving and maintaining his or her own sobriety, without reliance on any "Higher Power." SOS respects recovery in any form regardless of the path by which it is achieved. It is not opposed to or in competition with any other recovery programs.

SOS supports healthy skepticism and encourages the use of the scientific method to understand alcoholism.

---

*Reprinted with permission of the Secular Organizations for Sobriety. © by the Secular Organizations for Sobriety.

Afterword

Plant as many seeds of recovery as possible. It is not your business if and when these seeds grow — your task is to simply plant the seeds. As long as there is breath there is hope. Recovery is possible!

I hope *12-Step Programs: A Resource Guide for Helping Professionals* is helpful to you. As I found during my research, some of the programs seem to be well-kept secrets. Many of the programs I only found because I knew someone who was a member. If you know of any 12-step programs that are not listed, please share that information with me, in care of the publisher.

I would also appreciate any comments you may have regarding this edition of *12-Step Programs: A Resource Guide for Helping Professionals.*